BU

Dan Colwell

asi digoo evim. net (Maccoi)

JPMGUIDES

Contents

This Way Budapest

By the Blue Danube

Hungary's cosmopolitan capital sits spectacularly astride the Danube, the Buda Hills rising on one side and pancake-flat Pest spreading on the other. From every angle there are magnificent views. When you are in Pest, you'll find your eyes are drawn irresistibly upwards to the magnificent Buda skyline, topped with domes, spires and statues. From the top of Buda's Gellért Hill or Castle Hill, you'll be treated to unforgettable bird's-eye perspectives on the sprawling city down below.

Yet Budapest has many more sides to it than this. The tranquil streets of Buda's medieval Castle Hill district retain the ambience of another, quieter age, while the great boulevards of downtown Pest epitomize the elegance of bourgeois life in Central Europe at the end of the 19th century. Váci utca, Pest's main shopping street, buzzes with the latest trends, from haute couture to cyber cafés, and is most definitely part of the modern world.

Legacy of the Past

This ability to move with the times while holding on to the best of the past stems from Budapest's turbulent history of war and invasion. Certainly, the city has long had the knack of keeping what it likes from its foreign rulers, even when it has done its utmost to be rid of them. More than three centuries after the Ottomans were thrown out, Budapest is still famous for its splendid Turkish baths. And although the Austrians have come and gone, there are times when the city seems more Viennese than Vienna: the Habsburg palace on Castle Hill, the gleaming gilt of the fin-de-siècle Opera House, ladies in fur coats partaking of their afternoon *sachertorte* and coffee in venerable 19th-century cafés. And with the Danube flowing through its centre, you can't help feeling that this is a city where the sound of Johann Strauss's famous waltzes ought to fill the streets.

Whether the faces it shows are modern or medieval, Eastern or Austrian, one thing is certain—Budapest is Hungarian at heart. It has been the centre of the nation's cultural and political life for seven centuries, the seat of Hungary's kings, and home to its deepest aspirations to national liberty in the face of foreign oppression. The music you'll hear on the street has its roots planted in Hungarian soil.

Millennium Capital

Budapest jumped the gun in celebrating the millennium— 104 years early, to be exact. The first Magyar tribes had arrived in Hungary in 896, bringing with them their unique language, horse-riding skills and goulash recipes. One thousand years on found their descendants in a rare period of security and affluence—Hungary had recently achieved equal status with its erstwhile Austrian rulers in what was known as the Dual Monarchy—and they intended to celebrate their national Millennium in style.

They did so in one of the most lavish building sprees ever seen in a European capital. Many of Budapest's great set pieces were commissioned with the 1896 millennium in mind, and they have become its best-known sights. The Fishermen's Bastion and the revamped Matthias Church went up in Buda. On the Pest side, St Stephen's Basilica, the stunning Art Nouveau Museum of Applied Arts, Heroes' Square, the City Park and the mighty Parliament were built to honour the occasion. Even the M1 metro line was conceived as part of the celebrations.

Never ones to do anything by halves, the Hungarians entered the year 2000 with two more millennia to mark—not just Y2K itself, but more importantly that of the coronation of King Stephen on Christmas Day 1000. And by a happy coincidence, this finds them once again in an upbeat frame of mind about the future of the nation.

The Hungarian Way

For chefs the world over, *à la hongroise* means only one thing —the use of Hungary's most famous product, paprika. But doing things the Hungarian way could equally imply an exceptional creativity. This small country of only 10 million people has given birth to a surprisingly high proportion of great inventors, Nobel Prize winners, musicians and film makers, from József Biró, who invented the ballpoint pen, to the conductor Sir Georg Solti, publisher Joseph Pulitzer, actors Béla Lugosi and Tony Curtis and Oscar-winning directors George Cukor, Michael Curtiz and István Szabó. Not to mention Estée Lauder and Kalvin Klein! Like Budapest-born Harry Houdini, they were all escapologists of a sort, and had to leave their homeland to become famous—or simply remain free from persecution. Now that Hungary enjoys a less dangerous political climate it may be that luminaries of the future will be able to stay in the country that first nourished their talent.

The Parliament sits in neo-Gothic splendour on the bank of the Danube.

Taking the Waters

Their country may be land-locked, but when Hungarians want to relax they will be found sailing on, swimming in, or sunning themselves beside, any available stretch of water. Budapest itself has countless springs running beneath it, providing thermal waters for the city's many Turkish baths, open-air pools and health spas. For a pleasant trip beyond the capital, cruise slowly up the Danube to some of the nation's most beautiful old towns, such as the charming little town of Szentendre, the medieval royal seat of Esztergom or the clifftop fortress at Visegrád. Alternatively, enjoy the bright lights and serious tans of the Hungarian Riviera, as Lake Balaton likes to think of itself. In summer, every Friday evening, Budapest empties of its inhabitants as long streams of traffic head southwest to weekend cottages and bustling resorts surrounding this great expanse of warm, shallow water. The long, scenic lake stands in as the nation's seaside. Fishermen angle for pike-perch from boats or platforms protruding from the reeds. Others swim, windsurf, go yachting or just take it easy on the beach.

Flashback

Early History

Human traces have been found dating back to 500,000 BC. By the 3rd century BC, the area was inhabited by both Illyrians and the Eravisci, a Celtic tribe who occupied Gellért Hill on the Buda side of the Danube. The Roman army arrived in 35 BC and easily conquered the region, incorporating it into the Roman Empire after 14 BC under the name Pannonia.

It took just 20 years for the Pannonians to revolt against Roman rule. The uprising was soon put down, and the province carved in two. Aquincum—the Roman settlement just to the north of present-day Budapest—became the capital of Lower Pannonia and developed into an affluent provincial town.

Arrival of the Magyars

By 395 AD the Roman Empire was disintegrating under repeated attacks from barbarian forces, and Roman troops withdrew from Pannonia. The region soon became subject to invasion from a succession of Germanic and Slav tribes, such as the Huns, Bulgars and Avars, who dominated the Hungarian plains throughout the 7th and 8th centuries. Charlemagne's Holy Roman Empire took over in 800, and the territory was ruled by his successors for the rest of the century.

In 896—one of the most celebrated dates in Hungarian history—Magyar tribes from the area between the Urals and the River Volga crossed the Carpathian Mountains and set up home in the fertile plains of the Carpathian Basin. Their leader, Árpád, established a powerful dynasty that was to last for three centuries. Under his immediate successors, however, the Magyars went on the rampage around Europe, raiding as far as France and Spain, and were only stopped in 955 by the armies of the German emperor Otto I.

From this moment they began to give up their wild ways. Árpád's great-grandson, Géza, was received into the Western (Roman) Church in 975. The main job of converting the nation was left to his son, Stephen (István) I, crowned king on Christmas Day 1000 at Esztergom. This date marked Hungary's entrance into European statehood, sharing its Western neighbours' religious, political and cultural outlook. Stephen was later made a saint for his efforts in bringing his country into the Christian fold.

Medieval Budapest

The Árpád dynasty maintained a system of absolute monarchy, bolstered by a council of the nation's magnates. In 1222, the magnates decided they'd had enough monarchical bullying and forced the king, Andrew (András) II, into issuing the Golden Bull, a Hungarian version of the Magna Carta outlining the rights of nobles and commoners in relation to the monarch. A new assembly met in what is now Pest, giving the small town a major boost.

Sadly, this example of constitutional maturity came just as the country was about to lurch into crisis. In 1241–42, Mongol hordes descended on Hungary and devastated the cities. Afterwards, the energetic King Béla IV rebuilt the nation, establishing a series of defensive castles. The one on Buda Hill soon became the most important in the land, a pre-eminence it would never relinquish.

Andrew III, the last Árpád king, died without issue in 1301, and the throne was offered to Charles Robert of the French House of Anjou. Both he and his son, Louis I, extended Hungary's power and prosperity, but once again, foreign invasion threatened the nation. The Turks inflicted a disastrous defeat on King Sigismund in 1396. It was left to a Transylvanian nobleman, János Hunyadi, to reverse the setbacks some 50 years later, leading the Hungarians to victory in Belgrade.

His son, Matthias (Mátyás) Corvinus, became king in 1458. An enlightened tyrant, soldier, linguist, patron of the arts and founder of one of the biggest libraries in Europe, Matthias was Hungary's true Renaissance prince. His 32-year reign saw the Royal Palace on Buda Hill become one of the most important courts in central Europe. Yet, as so often proved the case, Hungary's cultural resurgence was short-lived. After Matthias's death, the country fell into civil unrest, with violent struggles developing between nobles and peasants. Meanwhile, just across the border in Serbia, the Turkish forces were gathering for a final onslaught. The Hungarians met them at the Battle of Mohács in 1526; they were decimated, and the king, Louis II, drowned trying to escape. The Turks entered Budapest on September 10 and sacked the town before withdrawing. Following further internal Hungarian political wrangling, they returned in 1541 and occupied the city for the next 145 years.

Turks and Habsburgs

With the Turkish army in Budapest, the Austrian Habsburgs moved into the western part of

Hungary to create a buffer state, while a remnant of the independent nation survived in the northern region of Transylvania. Hungary was effectively partitioned. Budapest became a Turkish garrison town, with its churches turned into mosques, an armoury and a number of Turkish baths.

The 17th century saw the Turks at the height of their power, culminating in the siege of Vienna in 1683. But their failure to take the city led to the swift collapse of Turkish morale. With Prince Eugene of Savoy at its head, the Habsburg army routed them in a series of battles, liberating Budapest in 1686, although the six-week siege left the city in ruins.

It soon became apparent to the Hungarians that, far from being liberated, they had merely exchanged one foreign dictatorship for another. In 1703, a nationalist rebellion began under Ferenc Rákóczi, but its defeat eight years later meant that Hungary was now effectively recognized as part of the Habsburg Empire.

The rest of the century saw Budapest develop into a classic Habsburg city, with a flourishing nobility patronizing its new theatres, baroque churches and palaces. At the same time, various ethnic groups from around the empire were encouraged to settle. As the city began to benefit from Habsburgian peace and economic prosperity, Austrian culture and the German language came to dominate the nation. This was not lost on a new breed of Hungarian nationalists frequenting the coffee houses of Pest and inspired by contemporary events such as the French Revolution of 1789. They smouldered with a passionate desire to rejuvenate the language and culture. Coupled with the increasing poverty of Hungary's peasant population, the country entered the 19th century in a combustible mood.

From Revolution to Dual Monarchy

The first effect of Hungary's renewed sense of national and cultural identiy came to be known as the Reform. Traditionally the Hungarian Parliament was a forum for the nobility, but it became filled with noticeably more democratic-minded members. One of them, Count István Széchenyi, was instrumental in modernizing Budapest and oversaw the construction of the first bridge across the Danube. But where Széchenyi believed Hungary could reinvent itself within the empire, for his younger colleagues in the Diet a more dramatic solution seemed to be the only way forward.

Clattering through the city, the yellow trams are the most practical way of getting around.

Things came to a head in 1848, the year of revolution all over Europe, when Viennese power wavered and a group of young intellectuals, including the nationalist poet Sándor Petőfi, led a bloodless coup in Budapest. An independent liberal Hungarian government was set up under such luminaries as Lajos Batthyány, Lajos Kossuth and Ferenc Deák, but it was inevitable that the Habsburg Empire would not let this challenge to its authority go unanswered. The first attempt to reconquer Hungary was beaten off by an improvised national army. However, a year after the revolution, the Habsburg emperor appealed to the Russian tsar for help, and although the Hungarians resisted with considerable tenacity, the combined opposing forces were far too strong. The premier, Kossuth, fled and the reinstatement of Viennese rule brought savage reprisals against the nationalists.

But Hungary's spirit was never broken. By 1867, the Austrians were again facing a crisis in their hold on the empire and, following a defeat by the Prussian army, sought to placate the Hungarians by offering them their own government and recognizing the equal status of the

Hungarian monarchy. The settlement is known as the Dual Monarchy.

Budapest flourished under the new Austro-Hungarian regime, benefiting in particular from favourable tariff agreements between the two countries. The constituent parts of the city—Buda, Pest and Óbuda—were officially united in 1873, and the construction of the grand boulevards, Opera House, metro and Parliament all testify to this being its golden age.

World War

The good times were not to last. The very fact of Hungary's hard-won equality in the empire meant that when World War I broke out, it was expected to shoulder a significant part of the burden. As a consequence, it suffered a remarkably high proportion of the casualties and, as the main ally of Germany, paid a heavy price when the Allied powers were victorious in 1918. The Habsburg Empire collapsed immediately, and Hungary entered one of its all-too-frequent periods of political turmoil. A bourgeois democratic republic was set up under Count Mihály Károlyi, soon to be replaced by Béla Kun's communist state. This in turn dissolved, leading to a right-wing takeover under Admiral Miklós Horthy in 1920.

Of more concern at the time was the harsh post-war peace treaty. Under the 1920 Treaty of Trianon, the nation lost a third of its population and almost 75 per cent of its territory to neighbouring countries, including the historically symbolic Transylvania, the preserver of Hungarian culture during the years of Turkish rule. During the inter-war period, Hungary struggled on through economic depression, although Budapest managed to keep up a reputation as a hangout for Western bohemians and artists.

World War II saw Hungary on the losing side again. The disastrous dalliance with Nazi Germany was due not only to their leaders' shared political outlook, but also an obsessive determination to regain the lands lost under the Trianon treaty, which Germany fostered by rewarding it with Transylvania. Nemesis came in the shape of the Red Army.

The Hungarians were routed supporting their allies at Stalingrad. When Horthy proclaimed an armistice, the Germans invaded Hungary. The ensuing Russian siege of Budapest, which lasted from December 1944 to February 1945, devastated the city, and the final defeat of the German and Hungarian forces ushered in a new era of Soviet sway in Hungary.

Behind the Iron Curtain

An initial attempt at democracy was made when, in November 1945, relatively free elections were held. The results were not to Moscow's liking, however, and by 1949 Hungary was declared a People's Republic with the pro-Stalin Mátyás Rákosi in power, backed up by the ÁVO secret police.

The 1950s proved to be a decade of economic depression and political repression. The result, in October 1956, was a popular uprising of workers and students. A provisional government under Imre Nagy withdrew from the Warsaw Pact and declared neutrality. But this was a step too far. Soviet tanks reentered Budapest and crushed the revolt. Nagy was executed, many others were deported to the Soviet Union and 200,000 Hungarians fled to the West.

The new Soviet appointee was János Kádár, who at first seemed to be an old-style communist leader. But although Hungary continued along its grim path for some years, in the mid-1960s the Kádár government began to foster a more liberal version of communism, allowing Hungarians to travel abroad and even encouraging a limited form of capitalism, known locally as the "goulash economy". This took Hungary into new areas of liberty and well beyond what was happening in the Soviet Union and other Eastern bloc countries at the time. It was no surprise, therefore, that the first chinks in the Iron Curtain were seen in Hungary when, in March 1989, a huge demonstration against the political regime led to the opening of borders with Austria. In October, the People's Republic finally collapsed.

Budapest Today

The transformation since 1989 has been astonishing. A market economy is in place, and the nation's gaze is fixed firmly westwards. Hungary joined NATO in 1999—an alliance sorely tested by the Kosovo campaign against Serbia, which has a large Hungarian minority. The general election in April 2002 was won, only just, by the Socialist Party (MSZP) under Peter Medgyessy, who formed a coalition government with the SZDSZ (Alliance of Free Democrats). Hungary became a member of the European Union in May 2004.

It's no exaggeration to say that with the affluence and sense of independence that has stemmed from this, and with its coffee houses and boulevards buzzing with an energy and optimism not seen for a century, Budapest is witnessing a new golden age.

Sightseeing

Buda and Pest remain very different in character, and you will find yourself happily enjoying the best of both worlds, alternating between the historic, medieval streets of Buda's Castle Hill and the bustling 19th-century boulevards of downtown Pest.

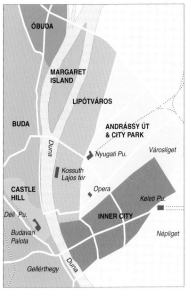

CASTLE HILL

Várhegy, a narrow plateau 60 m (197 ft) above the Danube, was for centuries the political and cultural centre of the nation, the seat of Hungary's kings and the home of its aristocracy and artisans. Its fantastic overview of the river and Pest plains also made it strategically vital for whoever wanted to control the region. Almost every invader who came this way over the course of 700 years attacked and destroyed it. It was rebuilt each time, and today it's virtually impossible to detect traces of its violent history.

Castle Hill has long given up its lofty royal authority to the energetic democracy of Pest, but there's still plenty to enjoy up here. The south end is dominated by the magnificent Royal Palace, while the quiet medieval streets of the north end are a delight simply to wander around and soak up the atmosphere. You can reach Castle Hill by the funicular, which starts from the Buda side of the Chain Bridge, the Várbusz shuttle bus from near Moszkva tér metro station, or under your own steam, via one of the many stairways leading up. Cars, however, are banned for non-residents other than guests at the Hilton Hotel.

Funicular

I. Szent György tér B 5*
Open daily 7.30 a.m.–10 p.m., closed every second Monday from 7.30 a.m.–3 p.m.

The funicular (*sikló*) reaches Castle Hill just north of the Royal Palace gates. It provides en route one of the shortest but most scenic rides in Budapest, climbing slowly up the hill from the riverside near the Chain Bridge in just a couple of minutes. The funicular has been in operation since 1870, the original steam engine only giving way to electricity in 1986.

Royal Palace

Budavári Palota B 5

The original castle was built on this site in 1242 by Béla IV following the Mongol devastation. It reached its peak of fame two centuries later when King Matthias made it one of Europe's great Renaissance courts. Left dilapidated after 145 years of Ottoman rule, it was rebuilt under the Habsburgs as a baroque palace, only to be destroyed in the epic Soviet onslaught against the Nazi garrison in 1945. Post-war reconstruction has seen it turned into the home of three excellent—

*References correspond to the fold-out map at the end of the guide.

and vast—museums. On top of the palace gates, Gyula Donáth's great sculpture of a huge eagle-like creature *(turul)* with wings outstretched looks out across the Danube. Hungarian mythology has it that the fierce-looking *turul* was the ancestor of Árpád, the nation's first king. Hungarians view it as their symbolic protector.

Budapest History Museum

Budapesti Történeti Múzeum B 5
I. Buda Palace Wing E
Mar–Oct daily 10 a.m.–6 p.m.,
Nov–Feb daily (except Tues)
10 a.m.–6 p.m.

At the southern tip of the palace complex, this interesting and informative museum looks at the history of the city since the Bronze Age. Head downstairs to the excavated part of the medieval castle, where there are the remains of Matthias's Royal Chapel and a striking roomful of Gothic statues unearthed in 1974. On the first floor, the fascinating Budapest in Modern Times exhibition examines the Habsburg period to the fall of communism. The top floor has gold, bracelets and other finds from both the Roman era and that of the later Barbarian tribes such as the Avars.

Hungarian National Gallery

Magyar Nemzeti Galéria B 5
I. Buda Palace, Wings B, C and D
Tues–Sun 10 a.m.–6 p.m.

Few of the artists on display will be known to foreign visitors, but this gigantic collection constitutes a

CARD DEALS

Avid culture-vultures and dedicated sightseers will find the **Budapest Card** well worth considering. For 5,200 Ft for two days or 6,500 Ft for three days, one adult and one child under 14 will gain admission to all the major museums and art galleries, as well several other sights such as the Budapest Zoo and the Vidám amusement park. It also offers unlimited travel on public transport and many reductions in shops, on sightseeing tours, car hire and the Airport Minibus. Cards can be obtained at hotels, museums, tourist offices and travel agencies. If you intend to travel further than Budapest, you might also like to invest in a **Hungary Card**, which offers reduced rates on the Hungarian Railways, Volán coaches, Mahart Balaton Shipping, Főtaxi and 6x6 Taxi, reductions in motorway tolls, discounts of 5 to 30% on hotel rooms and restaurant bills, free entry to various museums and national parks and reductions for cultural events. The card is valid for 13 months, recommended retail price is 5,520 Ft—and it also gives you a 20% reduction on the price of a Budapest Card. For more information, see http://www.miwo.hu

near-exhaustive account of Hungarian art across seven centuries. Highlights of the earlier period include some superb 15th-century paintings and a group of dazzling late-Gothic winged altarpieces. More modern works reflect mainstream European artistic trends, moving from Romanticism and Realism to Abstract. There's a remarkable range of Hungarian Impressionists, look out for names such as Rippl-Rónai, Kárdy and Kernstok, and startling modernists: Lajos Gulácsy, János Vaszary and Lajos Tihanyi. The museum is entered from the terrace overlooking the Danube, where you'll also find a fine equestrian statue of Eugene of Savoy, leader of the Habsburg forces that chased out the Turks in 1686.

Museum of Contemporary Art (Ludwig Collection)

I. Buda Palace Wing A   B 5
Tues–Sun 10 a.m.–6 p.m.

Works by famous international artists, including Picasso, Baselitz, Lichtenstein and Warhol, rub shoulders with those by home-grown talent such as Endre Tót, Molnár, Bak and Erdély. The link between them is of course their spirited subversion of traditional Western art, though with the museum rotating its huge collection and putting on temporary exhibitions, you can never be sure which artists' work will be delivering the shock of the new at any one time.

Dísz tér   B 5

Here you'll find one of the district's few dramatic reminders of how things looked after World War II— the former Ministry of Defence, whose bullet-riddled walls stand as a stark memorial to the last-ditch battle between the German and Russian armies in 1945.

Labyrinth of Buda Castle

Budavári Labirintus A 5
I. Úri utca 9
Open daily 9.30 a.m.–7.30 p.m.

Descend through a small doorway on Úri utca, north from Dísz tér, to this series of dank caves and dark tunnels. They were used as a place of refuge in medieval Buda, a World War II hospital and a Cold War military installation, but have now been saddled with unsuccessful waxworks and pretentious labyrinth routes. For all that, the labyrinth itself is a fascinating and undoubtedly creepy experience.

Multi-coloured glazed tiles add panache to Matthias Church.

Golden Eagle Pharmacy Museum

- Arany Sas Patikamúzeum A 5
- I. Tárnok utca 18
- In summer Tues–Sun
- 10.30 a.m.–5.30 p.m.

Tárnok utca, running parallel to Úri utca, contains several fine medieval buildings, not least the Golden Eagle, dating from the early 15th century but used as a pharmacy from around 1750 to just before World War I. There are lots of old chemist's jars and bottles, an alchemist's laboratory and displays on Buda's pharmaceutical history.

Matthias Church

- Mátyás templom A 4
- I. Szentháromság tér 2
- Mon–Sat 9.30 a.m.–5.30 p.m.,
- Sun 1 p.m.–5.30 p.m.
- (at other times for services)

The centre of Szentháromság tér (Trinity Square) has an early 18th-century votive column commemorating the end of a bubonic plague epidemic. But the whole scene is dominated by Matthias Church, in particular the riotous neo-Gothic fantasy of its spire and the striking multi-coloured roof. They were added as part of the church's extensive 19th-century restorations. Though dating originally from the 13th century, the church, like most of the district, has had a turbulent past. Named after King Matthias Corvinus, who was twice married here and who rebuilt it in the 1470s, it was later whitewashed and turned into a mosque by the Turks, only to be virtually flattened during the Habsburg siege of 1686.

The frescoed interior has a dark, appropriately medieval feel to it. On the left as you enter, the Loreto Chapel contains a highly valued red marble statue of the Virgin. Next to the altar, steps lead down to the crypt, which now houses the Museum of Ecclesiastical Art. Within its maze of narrow corridors are the church treasury, medieval carvings and the tomb of Béla III and his wife, the only one from the Árpád dynasty left untouched by the Ottomans.

Fishermen's Bastion

- Halászbástya A 4
- I. Szentháromság tér

Just behind Matthias Church, Fishermen's Bastion has faced accusations of being Disneyland kitsch—the turrets and statues of the bastion are as authentically medieval as the nearby Hilton Hotel—but that doesn't stop it having some of the best views of the city, as well as being very photogenic. It was put up between

1895 and 1902 by Frigyes Schulek as part of Budapest's building frenzy celebrating the 1,000th anniversary of the arrival of the Magyars in Hungary and matches the Gothic-style renovations of Matthias Church carried out by the same architect. The seven turrets represent the original seven Magyar tribes. In front of the bastion is an equestrian statue of Stephen, who as king and saint is adorned with both crown and halo and clutches the distinctive double cross.

Museum of Music History

Zenetörténeti Múzeum A 4
I. Táncsics Mihály utca 7
Tues–Sun 10 a.m.–6 p.m.

From Szentháromság tér, continue past the Hilton Hotel and bear right into what was the medieval Jewish quarter (the house at No. 26 served as a 14th-century synagogue). The charming music museum, located in a grand baroque mansion, has a fine musical pedigree—Beethoven stayed here in 1800. There's a superb collection of instruments, from lyres to Hungarian bagpipes, and musical memorabilia, including original manuscripts of Béla Bartók.

Museum of Commerce and Catering

Kereskedelmi és Vendéglátóipari Múzeum A 4
I. Fortuna utca 4
Wed–Fri 10 a.m.–5 p.m., Sat and Sun 10 a.m.–6 p.m.

Nearby Fortuna utca is an attractive street named after a famous 18th-century tavern. The tavern building has now been transformed into one of the city's most unusual and entertaining museums, belying its rather po-faced name.

Entered along a small alley, the Catering section to the left is a fascinating account of how Budapest's tourist industry boomed at the end of the 19th century, with mouth-watering displays showing the development of confectioner's shops, restaurants, coffee houses and grand hotels.

Opposite, the Commerce part of the museum covers the way Pest became the focus of Hungary's economic activity after the mid-19th century. Best of all are the lively exhibits on early advertising, including the city's first neon sign—a rickety 1926 beer advert which the attendant will switch on for you.

Telephone Museum

Telefónia Múzeum A 4
I. Úri utca 49
Tues–Sun 10 a.m.–4 p.m.

It's a little-known fact that the inventor of the telephone switchboard—Tivadar Puskás—

was Hungarian. Find out more about the nation's love affair with the telephone at this little museum on Úri utca.

Museum of Military History

Hadtörténeti Múzeum A 4
I. Tóth Árpád sétány 40
Apr–Oct Tues–Sun
10 a.m.–6 p.m.,
Nov–Mar 10 a.m.–4 p.m.

Continue walking away from the Danube and you'll come to Tóth Árpád sétány, the westernmost edge of Castle Hill where, from its quiet, leafy promenade, there are good views across to the Buda Hills. The museum is at the far end, located in a huge Habsburg-era barracks. With displays of uniforms, weapons, photos, paintings and waxworks, it is devoted to all things military: given Hungary's history, there's a lot to see. The exhibitions on the 1848 Revolution, the two World Wars and the 1956 Uprising are especially interesting, and ultimately the centuries of turmoil are placed in the context of the nation's peaceful achievement of democracy after 1989.

When you leave the museum, continue around to Anjou Bástya (bastion) for a historical curiosity, a memorial tablet marking the place of death of Abdurrahman Abdi Arnaut Pasha. He was the last Ottoman governor of Buda, killed in 1686 when the city was re-occupied and remembered with the inscription, "A valiant foe, may he rest in peace".

HURRAH FOR THE HUSSARS

It should come as no surprise that one of the few words the Hungarian language has given to the world is "Hussar". A flair for horsemanship is an integral part of the national character going back to the first Magyar tribes, who were famously adept in the saddle.

The Hussar light cavalry regiment was created under King Matthias in 1480 and became legendary throughout Europe for its bravery and devotion to homeland. By the time of the Napoleonic Wars there were Hussar brigades in every European army. But the best was yet to come. The Hussars entered nationalist myth when they sided with the Hungarian revolutionaries in 1848 and almost chased the Austrians out for good.

The nation takes great pride in its dashing Hussars to this day. Look out for the two memorials honouring them along Úri utca on Castle Hill, in particular the impressive statue of a 19th-century Hussar commander of the castle, András Hadik—seated on horseback, of course.

BUDA

Buda has a variety of great sights beyond Castle Hill. From Gellért Hill south of the Castle to Rózsadomb (Rose Hill) to the north, there are quiet parks and busy squares, Art Nouveau hotels and Soviet monuments, riverside walks and birds-eye views. Old districts such as Tabán—from the Turkish *tabahane,* or armoury—and Víziváros contain intriguing vestiges of Buda's Turkish occupation, including the city's best bathhouses. The Rózsadomb, meanwhile, is probably Budapest's most exclusive residential district, and its enormous villas have long been inhabited by Hungary's elite—though where once this meant Communist Party apparatchiks, now it's the nation's new ruling class of the rich and famous.

Gellért Hotel
and Baths Complex

- Gellért Szálló és Fürdő C 8
- Tram 18, 19, 47, 49
- XI. Szent Gellért tér 1
- Open Mon–Fri 6 a.m.–6 p.m.,
- Sat, Sun 6 a.m.–2 p.m.

This famous Art Nouveau hotel dominates the Buda side of the Szabadság híd (Liberty Bridge). Built between 1912 and 1918 on the site of an old Turkish bath, its sumptuous spa and swimming pool are probably the finest in the city. After the health treatment, reward yourself with coffee and cake at the elegant Gellért Eszpresszó.

Gellért Hill B–C 8

- Tram 18,19,47,49
- XI. Gellért-hegy

Opposite the Gellért baths, a small, steep path leads up to the 235-m (771-ft) hill, the site of a pleasant, peaceful park, with the Citadel, Liberation Monument and spectacular views of the Danube at the top. Almost immediately visible is the intriguing Cave Church (*Sziklatemplom*), consecrated under the Order of St Paul in 1926. The monks were arrested under the Communists in 1951, and the cave was bricked up until the order was re-established here in 1989.

Liberation Monument

- Szabadság szobor C 7
- XI. Gellért-hegy

A 14-m-high (46-ft) sculpture of a woman holding aloft a palm frond commemorates the Red Army's "liberation" of Budapest in 1945, and it's a rare example of Soviet-inspired statuary left in place after 1989. Perched right on top of the hill, she was of course too big a part of the Buda skyline simply to jettison, unlike the bronze Soviet

The historic Castle District in Buda is full of architectural surprises.

soldier who stood on the plinth below, consigned to Statue Park on the outskirts of the city (see p. 24).

Citadel

- Citadella C 7
- XI. Gellért-hegy

Just behind the monument is the severe-looking Citadel, built by the Austrians after the 1848 Revolution so they could keep an intimidating eye on their Hungarian subjects. The advent of the Dual Monarchy in 1867 made it redundant, and though as hated a symbol of foreign oppression as the Liberation Monument, it too survived.

Today, its walls enclose a hotel, restaurant and beer garden, and the panorama from the ramparts is extraordinary.

Gellért Monument B–C 7

- Tram 18, 19
- XI. Gellért-hegy

On the northern side of the hill, the great bronze statue of Bishop Gellért brandishes a cross at the river in which he died in 1046. An Italian missionary born in Venice, Gellért (Gerard) was stranded on the Dalmatian Coast on his way to the Holy Land. He settled in Hungary and was appointed tutor to Emeric, son of King Stephen, before becoming bishop of Csanád. After the king's death, the good bishop met his end when a mob of the unconverted put him in a barrel spiked with nails and hurled him down what is now Gellért Hill and into the Danube. The statue, dating from 1904, is situated in a small grotto with 12 columns, and stands above an artificial waterfall.

Rudas Baths
- Rudas Gyógyfürdő C 7
- Tram 18, 19
- I. Döbrentei tér 9
- Mon–Fri 6 a.m.–5 p.m., Sat and Sun 6 a.m.–midday.
- Baths men only. Pool open to men and women 6 a.m.–5 p.m.

These historic Turkish baths, located on the embankment near Erzsébet híd, were built in the 16th century by order of the Turkish pasha Sokollu Mustapha and retain their eastern ambience, with a stone Ottoman dome, octagonal main pool and hexagonal windows.

Semmelweis Museum of Medical History
- Semmelweis Orvostörténeti Múzeum B 6
- Tram 18
- I. Apród utca 1–3
- Tues–Sun 10.30 a.m.–5.30 p.m.

The medical scientist Ignác Semmelweis was born in 1818 in this neo-baroque house below the southern tip of Castle Hill. He became known as the "Saviour of Mothers" for discovering the reason for the high mortality rate of women contracting puerperal fever during childbirth. The museum has various items belonging to the doctor on display, as well as a fascinating array of archaic medical implements, and the entire Holy Spirit pharmacy, dating back to 1813 and originally located in Pest.

Batthyány Square B 4
- M2 Batthyány tér
- I. Batthyány tér

At the heart of the Víziváros district, a jumble of narrow streets leading down from the north end of Castle Hill to the river, bustling Batthyány Square is something of a transport hub, with a bus and tram terminus, metro, and the HÉV station for trains heading to Szentendre. That doesn't stop it being also one of the city's most attractive locations. On its open, river side, the view across to the Parliament is unparalleled. But it also has some of Buda's finest 18th-century architecture.

The former White Cross Inn, dating from 1770, has a splendid sloping roof and was once the favourite watering hole of those using the Viennese stagecoach, which terminated nearby. It's now called **Casanova House** in honour of the Italian rake who legend has it once stayed here.

But by far the most striking baroque structure on the square, indeed some think in the whole city, is undoubtedly **St Anne's Church** (*Szent Anna templom*), designed by a Jesuit, Ignatius Pretelli, in Italian style in the mid-18th century—note the eye-in-the-triangle symbol on the gable between the two magnificent towers. The interior is a dazzling baroque drama of huge statues and black marble columns.

Király Baths

Király Gyógyfürdő B 3
M2 Batthyány tér
Tram 4, 6
II. Fő utca 84
Men: Tues, Thurs, Sat 9 a.m.– 7 p.m.; Women: Mon, Wed, Fri 7 a.m.–6 p.m.

FALLEN IDOLS

It takes some effort to get to **Statue Park** but it's more than worth it, for here is proof that discredited old statues don't die—they live on as entertainment for the next generation. When Hungary was under communist rule, Budapest's main squares were filled with typically unsubtle examples of the prevailing Soviet aesthetic—massive figures of Marx and Lenin, outsized sculptures of Party leaders and heroic-looking workers—all intended to remind the citizens of Budapest who was in control, and all thoroughly loathed. With the collapse of communism in 1989 their days were numbered. But rather than being smashed up, many have managed to eke out an honourable retirement tucked away in a field in Buda XXII.

This unique outdoor museum opened in 1993 and maintains a subtle balance between irony and historical respect. Here, among many relics of the Cold War years, you'll find the flag-bearing Soviet soldier from the base of the Liberation Monument on Gellért Hill, Imre Varga's striking Béla Kun memorial, and 4-m-high (13-ft) statues of Karl and Vladimir to welcome you at the entrance. The excellent museum catalogue tells you about the statues and where in Budapest they were originally located.

Statue Park is open daily from May to October, 10 a.m. to 6 p.m., and in winter from 10 a.m. till dusk. To get there, take the special bus from Deák tér (departures November to February at 11 a.m.; March to June, September and October at 11 a.m. and 3 p.m.; July and August 11 a.m., 3 and 4 p.m.).

Reminders of communist days have been relegated to the Szoborpark south-west of Buda on the way to Diósd.

Continue north along the main road to another of Buda's atmospheric Turkish baths, with trademark octagonal pool and stone dome. This one dates from 1565 and was located inside the town's defensive walls to ensure that the troops could bathe even if there was a siege going on outside.

The museum lies a couple of blocks west of the baths, and is located in the original 19th-century foundry set up by Swiss industrialist Abraham Ganz at the start of Hungary's industrial revolution. It gives an insight into the nitty-gritty of how the modern city, from trams to street lamps, was constructed in metal works such as this.

Foundry Museum
- Öntödei Múzeum B 3
- M2 Batthyány tér
- Tram 4, 6
- II. Bem József utca 20
- Tues–Sun 10 a.m.–5 p.m.

Tomb of Gül Baba
- Gül Baba Türbéje A 2
- Tram 4, 6
- II. Mecset utca 14
- May–September Tues–Sun
- 10 a.m.–6 p.m.

Gül Baba was a Turkish dervish killed during the siege of Buda in 1541, and his simple, green-domed tomb can be found just beyond busy Margit Körút in a beautifully tranquil location, on a small hill in the upmarket Rózsadomb district.

Béla Bartók Memorial House
: Bartók Béla Emlékház (off map)
: Bus 5
: II. Csalán utca 29
: Tues–Sun 10 a.m.–5 p.m.

Pick up the bus at Moszkva tér and head out through the posh Rózsadomb suburbs to what was the composer's last home in Hungary before his self-imposed exile in the United States in 1940. In front of the house stands a statue of Bartók by Imre Varga, the country's best-known modern sculptor. You can see Bartók's study, as well as photos and displays covering his life and career, including the Edison phonograph with which he travelled around the country in the early 20th century recording the country's folk music. The house has a small concert room where recitals are given on most Friday evenings—these are held outdoors in summer.

Buda Hills (off map)
Buda's extensive green hills provide a relatively cool, shady spot in summer, and the chance to get away from the noise and fumes of the city without too much effort. Indeed, the various means of transport that get you there are as much fun as the hills themselves. From opposite the Budapest Hotel, two stops west of Moszkva tér (A 3) by trams 18 and 56, you can take the 25-minute cog-railway ride to the top of Széchenyi-hegy. The hills here are great for hiking— and you might keep an eye out for wild boar and deer. A less energetic but equally pleasing way to enjoy the scenery is to take a trip on the marvellous narrow-gauge **Children's Railway**, reached across a small park from the cog-railway terminus. Apart from the drivers, this is operated entirely by children, a throwback to the days of communist youth groups (it used to be called the Pioneers' Railway). The trains wind through delightful woodland to János-hegy, the highest point in Budapest.

A 15-minute walk from here brings you to the Erzsébet Lookout Tower, with a spectacular bird's-eye view of the city and surrounding countryside.

For a blissfully peaceful descent, you can float down gently on the nearby chairlift (*libegő*). At the bottom, hop onto bus 158 back to Moszkva tér.

ÓBUDA

Just north of Buda, Óbuda occupies the site of Aquincum, the Roman capital of Lower Pannonia, and is thus the oldest part of the city (the name means simply Old Buda). The remains of the original Roman town are scattered throughout the district—there's an amphitheatre on the corner of Nagyszombat utca and Pacsirtamező út and military baths near the Árpád híd train station, for example—but they haven't been well maintained and today sit among busy roadways and flyovers. The calmest spot in which to dwell on the Roman past is at the Aquincum Museum. Afterwards, you can return to the delightful, cobbled squares of central Óbuda which, with their cafés, restaurants and galleries, are veritable oases within the concrete desert created by 1970s town planners.

Aquincum Museum
- Aquincumi Múzeum
- HÉV Aquincum
- III. Szentendrei út 139
- Tues–Sun 10 a.m.–5 p.m.; ruins open Apr–Oct 9 a.m.–5 p.m.

The site of Roman Aquincum's main civil town is 100 m (100 yards) south of the HÉV station. All that's left are the ruins of the civil amphitheatre and the foundations of villas, shops and the layout of the central areas. The museum displays excavated items, such as domestic utensils and musical instruments, as well as a model of what the town would have looked like.

Vasarely Museum
- HÉV Árpád híd
- III. Szentlélek tér 1
- Tues–Sun 10 a.m.–5.30 p.m.

Prepare to be dazzled. There are more than 350 works by Viktor Vasarely, one of the leading exponents of Op Art, where the spectator's eye is subject to optical illusions created through the use of stunning patterns and colours. The museum is in a fine old mansion just outside the station.

Imre Varga Museum
- Varga Imre Gyüjtemény
- HÉV Árpád híd
- III. Laktanya utca 7
- Tues–Sun 10 a.m.–6 p.m.

Behind delightful Főtér, and signalled by a group of Varga statues standing outside the entrance clutching umbrellas, this museum houses an impressive collection of powerful portraits and other works by Hungary's greatest modern sculptor.

MARGARET ISLAND

Margitsziget sits in the middle of the river between Buda and Pest, and its geography largely accounts for why the Romans founded a settlement in Budapest in the first place—they used the island as a stepping stone to make the passage from bank to bank less dangerous.

During the 13th century, King Béla IV founded a convent here, and vowed that if Hungary survived the Mongol invasions he would place his daughter in it. Hungary did—just—and Princess Margaret was duly packed off to the island that now bears her name, never to leave. The ruins of this Dominican convent (Domonkos kolostor romjai), including Margaret's burial place marked with a marble plaque, can be seen on the east side of the island.

It's still a haven of peace—private cars are, in the main, banned—and also the city's finest playground, where Budapestis go for regular doses of R&R, be it at the famous Palatinus thermal baths,

While the water soothes away their aches and pains, the Hungarians give their brain cells some exercise.

taking part in sports activities such as cycling and tennis, walking in the shade of the island's 10,000 trees or merely lying back in a quiet spot and enjoying the sunshine.

Palatinus Strand
- Tram 4, 6/bus 26
- XIII. Margitsziget
- Open daily May–Sept 8 a.m.–7 p.m.

Strands are an essential part of the Budapest summer, a place where urbanites can lounge by a pool or take a thermal bath in the company of large groups of fellow urbanites. This one can accommodate an astonishing 20,000 bathers in its seven cold- and warm-water pools and two children's pools, so it's probably as well that most people seem to prefer lounging to swimming.

Thermál Hotel Margitsziget
- Bus 26
- XIII. Margitsziget
- Open daily 7 a.m.–8 p.m.

At the northern end of the island, this ultramodern hotel is located on an old spa—Margaret Island is famously awash with hot mineral springs that fuel the curative baths here—and has three thermal pools, two swimming pools and two single-sex saunas. The waters are said to be good for every ailment from slipped discs to rheumatism.

INNER CITY

Belváros comprises the oldest part of Pest. Its layout dates back to medieval times, though what you see today is mainly the result of a huge reconstruction programme in the late 19th century. The line of what were once the city walls is now marked by the bustling roads of the Kiskörút (the Little Boulevard, consisting of Károly körút, Múzeum körút and Vámház körút). Within this area is Pest's liveliest streetlife, most notably around the famous Váci utca.

Vigadó Square C 6
: M1 Vörösmarty tér
: Tram 2

This lively waterfront square contains the superb Vigadó theatre and craft stalls, and offers an attractive view across to Buda. Boats leave from here for Danube Bend river trips.

Vörösmarty Square C 5
: M1 Vörösmarty tér

Fountains, regular markets, buskers and street performers, an ice-cream stand—try the marzipan flavour, or egg nog, or the one with chopped up Mozartkugeln chocolates—and the venerable Gerbeaud patisserie, an elegant throwback to Habsburg Budapest, combine to make this large square one of Pest's most popular hangouts. It's also the terminus of the M1 Millennial Railway, built in 1896 to celebrate Hungary's 1,000th birthday. This was the first metro in continental Europe and, with its small carriages and brown-tiled stations, it retains a delightfully old-fashioned ambience.

Metro Museum
: Földalatti Múzeum C 5
: M1, M2, M3 Deák tér
: V. Deák tér metro station
: Tues–Sun 10 a.m.–6 p.m.

Head east from the square along Deák Ferenc utca to this small museum located inside the metro station. It fills in the background to the building of the Millennial Railway, and has an original 1896 carriage on display.

Váci utca C 5–D 7
: M1 Vörösmarty tér
: Tram 2

The city's premier shopping street leads south, parallel to the Danube, from Vörösmarty tér. It's totally pedestrianized and packed with shops selling Hungarian wine and food, art and antiques, cosmetics, fashion and jewellery. Street vendors hawk all manner of goods, from glamorous sunglasses to

On Szervita tér, the mosaic designed by Miksa Róth for the former Turkish Bank is entitled Glory to Hungary.

leather belts and embroidered tablecloths. If you have shopped till you dropped, there are several cafés and restaurants where you can sit back and contemplate the street's eclectic architectural mixture.

Inner City Parish Church

Belvárosi Plébánia templom C 6
M3 Ferenciek tere
V. Március 15 tér
Open daily 8 a.m.–7 p.m. Latin service on Sun at 10 a.m.

Nestled against the busy flyover leading to Elizabeth Bridge, Pest's oldest building has a decidedly inner city location. The church was founded in the 12th century but destroyed by the Mongols, and though the façade is pure baroque, the interior, especially the fan-vaulted sanctuary around the altar, retains the Gothic beauty of its 14th-century reconstruction. The church was turned into a mosque during Turkish rule, and a *mihrab*, an Islamic prayer niche, can be seen near the altar.

In the square outside the church are the remains of Contra-Aquincum, a Roman fort which served as an outpost of the main settlement at Aquincum.

Paris Arcade

Párizsi Udvar D 6
M3 Ferenciek tere
V. Ferenciek tere 10–11

Near the church, on either side of
Kossuth Lajos utca, are the
distinctive Klotild mansions and,
beyond them, this extravagant Art
Nouveau shopping arcade,
completed in 1913. The gold-leaf
mosaics and Eastern motifs give it a
richly exotic, Byzantine look—it's
hard to believe it began life as the
mundane-sounding Inner City
Savings Bank.

Central Synagogue

Nagy Zsinagóga D 5–6
M2 Astoria
VII. Dohány utca 2

Daily (except Saturday)
10 a.m.–5 p.m.

Continue along Kossuth Lajos utca
to Károly körút, where the twin
onion-domed towers of the huge
main synagogue are soon visible.
It's the biggest synagogue in
Europe, built in oriental-Byzantine
style in 1859 and able to hold
3,000 worshippers. It has recently
been restored to its original
splendour, funded in part by a
foundation set up by Hollywood
actor Tony Curtis, whose parents
emigrated from Hungary in the
1920s.

During World War II, the Nazis,
aided by Hungarian Arrow Cross
fascists, used the synagogue as a
detention camp. Thousands of Jews

PORCELAIN

High-quality Hungarian arts and crafts have a long history, especially in
ceramics and porcelain. Items made from these materials have become the
most sought-after products for visitors to Hungary. Two names in particular
stand out. The Herend Porcelain Factory is based in the town of Herend near
Lake Balaton and has been making exquisite hand-painted vases, dishes,
bowls and statuettes since 1826. Herend has proved especially popular with
royalty—satisfied customers include Queen Victoria, Kaiser Wilhelm I, the
Shah of Iran and Prince Charles. Find out why at the main Herend shop just
behind Vörösmarty tér on V. József Nádor tér 11.

Zsolnay porcelain might not be able to boast as famous a client list, but
its products have been far more prominently placed. The company developed a line in brilliant weatherproof ceramic tiles in the late 19th century,
and these adorn the rooftops of Matthias Church, the Central Market and
the Museum of Applied Arts. Check out their modern Art Nouveau-influ-
enced designs at V. Kígyó utca 4.

died here and in the nearby ghetto. Many are buried in the adjoining Garden of Remembrance. Imre Varga's moving **Holocaust Memorial**, a weeping willow made of metal, has the family names of the dead etched onto its leaves.

Jewish Museum

- Zsidó Múzeum D 5–6
- M2 Astoria
- VII. Dohány utca 2
- Mon–Thurs 10 a.m.–3 p.m.,
- Fri, Sun 10 a.m.–2 p.m.

The museum is inside the synagogue complex, and occupies the site where Theodor Herzl, the founder of Zionism, was born in 1860. The rooms are largely devoted to the history and customs of the Jewish religion and culture. Among the exhibits are medieval prayerbooks and a 3rd-century gravestone. One room is devoted to the terrible events of the Hungarian Holocaust and the fate of the Budapest ghetto.

Jewish Quarter D–E 5

The narrow, grimy streets of Pest VII's **Erzsébetváros** (Elizabeth Town) district spread out behind the Central Synagogue. During the 18th century they became the centre of Budapest's Jewish community—until that time Jews were prohibited from living in Pest and had made their home in Buda. The area was turned into a ghetto under the Nazis, when the entire Jewish population was effectively imprisoned here behind hastily built walls. Up to 700,000 had been murdered by the time the Red Army arrived in 1945.

The area has managed to retain its Jewish character despite the wartime catastrophe. Apart from the mighty Central Synagogue, there are a number of other synagogues in the vicinity, as well as Jewish restaurants and kosher pastry shops, for example the venerable **Fröhlich Cukrászda** on Dob utca.

On the same street, be sure to take a look at the intriguing **Carl Lutz memorial**. Lutz was a Swiss national stationed as head of the embassy department for the representation of foreign nationals. From 1942 he helped obtain permits for Hungarian Jews to immigrate to Israel. In this way he saved over 62,000 people from the danger of deportation to concentration camps. Lutz never had the glory of Raoul Wallenberg, his Swedish counterpart, though the memorial is intended to redress this. It shows an angel emerging from the side of a wall to aid a fallen victim.

Hungarian National Museum

- Magyar Nemzeti Múzeum D 6
- M3 Kálvin tér
- VIII. Múzeum körút 14–16
- Tues–Sun
- 10 a.m.–6 p.m.

Just north of the subway station you'll see the magnificient neoclassical façade of the National Museum. It was from here on March 15 1848—just a year after the museum opened—that Hungary's great nationalist poet Sándor Petőfi read aloud his *National Song* and, effectively, launched the revolution against Habsburg rule.

The huge—and hugely interesting—exhibition is imaginatively designed and covers the entire drama of the nation's history, from the settlement of the Magyars in the Carpathian Basin to the collapse of communism and advent of democracy more than a thousand years later.

The beautiful Hungarian crown jewels are the highlight of the fabulous collections. They are displayed separately in their own darkened room. These are said to

Onion domes topping Moorish-style minarets dominate the Great Synagogue, built by Ludwig Förster.

have been used at the coronation of King Stephen in 1000, but probably date from slightly later—the lower part of the crown is thought to be Byzantine, from around the 1070s, while the upper part is possibly Hungarian Gothic of a century later. Their history is as chequered as Hungary's—they were smuggled out of the country to escape the Mongols, at which time the crown's cross was bent, they were twice stolen, buried in Transylvania to stop the Habsburgs getting their hands on them and, after World War II, taken to Germany by Hungarian fascists to keep them away from the Communists. Seized by the US Army, they languished in Fort Knox until 1978, when they were finally allowed back to their homeland.

Serbian Orthodox Church

- Szerb templom D 7
- M3 Kálvin tér
- V. Szerb utca 2–4
- Sun 9.30 a.m.–2 p.m.

Follow Kecskeméti utca from Kálvin tér, and turn left onto Szerb utca, just before you reach the large baroque University Church. The fine Serbian Orthodox Church dates from the late 17th century and was paid for by Serb merchants and artisans, who lived in the area. Its interior is particularly beautiful, but can only be seen on Sunday mornings, when the church opens for High Mass.

Great Market Hall

- Nagy Vásárcsarnok D 7
- Tram 2, 47, 49
- IX. Vámház körút 1
- Mon–Fri 6 a.m.–6 p.m.,
  Sat 6 a.m.–2 p.m.

The Inner City's cavernous red-brick and cast iron market hall, at the end of Váci utca near Szabadság bridge, opened for business in 1897. The ground floor is crammed with food stalls selling every conceivable ingredient for the traditional Hungarian meal—meat, fish, vegetables, bread, cheese, tins of goose liver, little bags of paprika, stalactites of salami and huge garlands of garlic and cherry peppers. Upstairs are as many souvenir and novelty shops as you could want in one place. The prices are slightly cheaper than at souvenir stalls in the touristy villages.

Museum of Applied Arts

- Iparművészeti Múzeum E 7
- M3 Ferenc körút
- IX. Üllői út 33–37
- Tues–Sun 10 a.m.–6 p.m.

From Kálvin tér, head away from the Belváros district along Üllői út to the outer ring of boulevards known as the Nagykörut. Here you'll find this intriguing collection of arts and crafts objects, with pride of place going to the superb Art Nouveau items from the 1900 Paris Expo. But this is a museum where the building outshines the contents. Designed by Ödön Lechner for Hungary's 1896 millennial celebrations, it's a stunning Art Nouveau fantasy, with external oriental cupolas and green-and-gold Zsolnay roof tiles. The Moorish-style white interior with a vast glass ceiling is breathtaking.

Holocaust Memorial Centre

- Budapest Holokauszt Múzeum E 7
- M3 Ferenc körút
- IX. Páva út 39
- Tues–Sun 10 a.m.–6 p.m.

The memorial is based in a disused magnificently restored synagogue, and also includes a new complex of buildings with exhibition halls, offices, conference rooms and research centre. It is funded by the Hungarian government. The controversial permanent exhibition, From Deprivation of Rights to Genocide, shows how Hungarian Jews were persecuted in the decades before the Holocaust. You can also visit the synagogue and the temporary exhibitions, among them photos of Auschwitz.

LIPÓTVÁROS

The northern part of Pest V, Lipót-város (Leopold Town) is the city's financial and political district. Its squares are noticeably less intimate than those in Belváros, although grandiose Szabadság tér makes up for it by having some of Pest's finest Eclectic and Art Nouveau architecture. There are also two major buildings erected with the 1896 millennial celebrations in mind, the mighty Basilica and Hungary's spectacular Houses of Parliament, both of whose domes reach up a symbolic 96 m (315 ft) high.

St Stephen's Basilica
- Szent István Bazilika C 5
- M3 Arany János utca
- V. Szent István tér 33
- Mon–Sat 9 a.m.–7 p.m.,
- Sun 1–4 p.m.; treasury and
- Chapel of the Holy Right open
- Apr–Sep 9 a.m.–5 p.m.,
- Oct–Mar 10 a.m.–4 p.m.

This vast church is the biggest in Budapest, with a capacity—often reached—of 8,500 worshipers. The first attempt at building it was in 1851, but the dome collapsed in a storm. Miklós Ybl took over the reconstruction, completed in 1905, designing it in neo-Renaissance style with a massive central nave.

In a chapel next to the altar you can see the church's most revered relic—the mummified right hand of St Stephen (known as the Holy Right, or Szent Jobb) kept in a silver reliquary. Drop a coin in the slot to illuminate it.

Afterwards, shake off the gloom of the interior by ascending the dome for a magnificent view of the city.

Roosevelt Square C 5
- Tram 2
- V. Roosevelt tér

From the basilica, Zrínyi utca leads straight towards Roosevelt tér. The square is dominated by the remarkable Hammer-horror façade of **Gresham Palace**, built in 1906 for the London-based Gresham Insurance Society in Art Nouveau style. It faces the famous **Chain Bridge** (*Széchenyi Lánchíd*), the inspiration of that indefatigable modernizer Count Széchenyi. The bridge was designed by an English engineer, William Tierney Clark, and built by a Scotsman, Adam Clark. When it opened in 1849 it was the first ever permanent link between Buda and Pest. On the north side of the square is yet another of Széchenyi's brainchildren, the superb **Hungarian Academy of Sciences**, which he founded in 1825.

Liberty Square

- Szabadság tér C 4
- M3 Arany János utca
- V. Szabadság tér

Make your way back to Nádor utca and head north to Liberty Square, whose grand dimensions perfectly express Hungary's pretensions to Great Power status at the end of the 19th century. Laid out on the site of barracks, demolished in 1886, this was the empire's financial nerve centre.

The huge **Hungarian Television Building** (MTV) at No. 17 was originally the Stock Exchange, while the Art Nouveau **National Bank**, opposite at No. 9, served as the Central Bank before World War I. Other notable buildings include the lemon-coloured **US Embassy** at No. 12. Behind this, Ödön Lechner's amazing multi-gabled **Post Office Savings Bank** of 1901 exemplifies Hungarian Art Nouveau in full flow; the façades are decorated with flowers, leaves and tendrils while bees climb up the gables towards hive-like pinnacles that symbolize savings.

The **obelisk** in the centre of the square is a rare Soviet-era survivor, and commemorates Red Army soldiers who died in the siege of Budapest in 1945. It replaced the Monument to Hungarian Grief, which flew a flag permanently at half-mast to mark the disastrous Treaty of Trianon and had an inscription from Mussolini.

Parliament

- Országház C 3–4
- M2 Kossuth Lajos tér
- Tram 2
- V. Kossuth Lajos tér
- Guided Tours in English Mon–Fri 10 a.m., noon and 2 p.m. (tickets must be bought beforehand at Gate X)

The stunning neo-Gothic Parliament sits by the Danube like an exotic version of its counterpart in London. It was completed in 1902 and underlined Budapest's imperial status within the Austro-Hungarian Empire, although its massive size—there are 691 rooms most of which have never been used—meant it was always too big for the country's boots.

An enjoyable guided tour takes you via the magnificent main staircase to a central hall lined with statues of Hungary's past rulers and on to the debating chamber, outside which are numbered brass racks where members had to leave their cigars before entering. If the interior positively glitters, that's because it is covered in gold—60 kg (132 lb) worth, spread as thin as paint on columns, walls and ceilings.

Museum of Ethnography

- Néprajzi Múzeum C 3
- M2 Kossuth Lajos tér
- Tram 2
- V. Kossuth Lajos tér 12
- Daily (except Monday)
- Mar–Oct 10 a.m.– 6 p.m.,
- Nov–Feb 10 a.m.–5 p.m.

Across from the Parliament, the museum is located in the former Supreme Court building dating from 1896. Pass through a superb neo-baroque entrance hall and up to the first-rate main exhibition on the history and culture of rural Hungary—which, until relatively recently, meant virtually the entire country other than Budapest. There are also frequently held temporary exhibitions looking at other ethnic groups from around the world.

Palace of Wonders

- Csodák Palotája D 1
- M3 Lehel tér
- XIII. Váci út 19
- Mon–Fri 9 a.m.–5 p.m.,
- Sat and Sun 10 a.m.–6 p.m.

This fun-filled, hands-on, interactive science playhouse—the word "museum" is kept at a safe distance—will appeal to inquisitive minds of all ages. The exhibitions change regularly, but recent favourites have included a flight simulator on board a real MiG-15 in which you can test your flying skills and a sticky Velcro wall on which you can see what it's like to be a fly.

While you're in the area, be sure to take in the square's daily, and very lively, open-air food market.

RETURN OF A HERO

During World War II, Swedish diplomat Raoul Wallenberg worked tirelessly in the face of constant danger from Budapest's Nazi authorities to help their Jewish victims. He handed out passports to Jews, hid others in safe houses and distributed food to those waiting on trains to be deported. The estimate of lives saved ranges from 4,000 to 35,000, but his own life was to end tragically. Arrested as a spy by the Soviets soon after they reached Budapest, he died in a Moscow prison in 1947, though rumours persisted for many years that he was still alive. Wallenberg is honoured in Budapest by an Imre Varga sculpture on Szilágyi Erzsébet fasor in Buda and a superb Pál Pátzay statue in Szent István Park, by the Danube in Pest XIII. The statue was spirited away from the park in 1949 just before its official unveiling, probably because the Soviets were embarrassed by its presence. The ceremony eventually took place 50 years behind schedule in 1999, when the memorial was at last back in its rightful home.

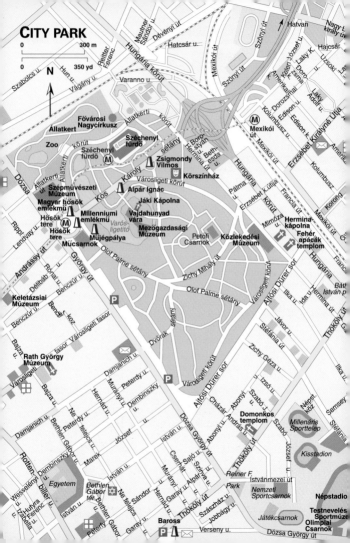

CITY PARK

0 — 300 m
0 — 350 yd

N

Szabolcs u.
Hun u.
Vágány u.
Mauner Sándor
Dévényi út
Reitter Ferenc
Hungária körút
Varanno u.
Hatcsár u.
Hatvan
Szőnyi út
Nagy L király u.
Hajcsár
Mexikói út
Kerepesi József út
Laky K u.
Doro
Lujzoki út
Dsma
Amerikai út
Dorozsma
Dozsma
Edison u.
Kolumbusz u.
Edison k.
Laky Adél u.
Erzsébet Királyné Útja
Ameri
Kolumbusz u.

Állatkert
Fővárosi Nagycirkusz
Állatkerti körút
Mexikói út
Állatkerti körút
Zoo
Széchenyi fürdő
Széchenyi fürdő
sétány
Boro
Hermina
Besda
Hungária körút
Mexikói út

Állatkerti út
Szépművészeti Múzeum
Kós
Károly
Városligeti körút
Zsigmondy Vilmos
Körszínház
Alpár Ignác
Palma
Erzsébet K útja
Franca út
Mexikói tér
Korong

Magyar hősök emlékmű
Hősök tere
Hősök tere
Millenniumi emlékmű
Városligetitó
Jáki Kápolna
Vajdahunyad vára
Mezőgazdasági Múzeum
Petőfi Csarnok
Közlekedési Múzeum
Erzsébet körút
Mimóza
Hermina-kápolna
Fehér apácák templom
Hungária

Dózsa
Rippl
Lenovay út
Műcsarnok
Műjégpálya
Olof Palme sétány
Zichy Mihály út
Olof Palme sétány
Városligeti körút
Ajtósi Dürer sor
Ilka u.
István p
Hermina út
Ida u.

Andrassy út
Délibab
Bajza
Rónai u.
Benczúr köz
György út
P
Bajza
Benczúr u.
Lendvay út
Zichy Géza út
Stefánia út
Jávor u.
Thököly út

Keletázsiai Múzeum
Benczúr u.
Bajza
Benda
Benda köz
Városligeti fasor
Dvórak
Zichy Géza út
Izsó u.
Stefánia út

Rath György Múzeum
Damjanich u.
Városligeti fasor
Muranyi u.
Peterdy u.
Dembinszky
P
Városligeti körút
Ajtósi Dürer sor
Chazár András u.
Abonyi u.
Szabó J
Izsó u.
Népst köz
Semsey
Stefánia

Damjanich u.
Bajza u.
Ne telefu u.
Peterdy u.
József
István u.
Abonyi u.
Dózsa György út
Szabó J
Domonkos templom
Millenáris Sporttelep
Kisstadion

Wesselényi
Dembinszky
Bethlen Gábor u.
Marek
Csernyo u.
Sajó u.
Muranyi u.
Szinva u.
Reiner F. Park
Istvánmezei út
Nemzeti Sportcsarnok
Népstadio

Ló utvea
Ferenc u.
Peterfy u.
Garay u.
Egyetem
Bethlen Gábor tér
Ne telefu
István u.
Bethlen Gábor u.
Cserha
Garay u.
István u.
Alpár u.
Dózsa György út
Thököly út
Istvánmezei út
Játékcsarnok
Testnevelési Sportmúzé Olimpiai Csarnok

Baross
Peterfy u.
Garay u.
Thököly út
Szász ház u.
jobbágy u.
Verseny u.
Dózsa György út

ANDRÁSSY ÚT AND CITY PARK

Two and a half kilometres long and straight as a die, Andrássy út is Budapest's magnificent riposte to the Champs-Elysées. The avenue was built in the 1870s and goes from near St Stephen's Basilica in the city centre out to City Park. The M1 metro line runs beneath it. If you choose to walk, be sure to note the emphatic eclecticism of its architecture—virtually every house has a different feature.

At its far end, City Park is the best in Budapest and packed with great things to do and see, including a mock-Transylvanian castle, circus, amusement park and zoo.

Postal Museum

Posta Múzeum D 4–5
M1 Bajcsy-Zsilinszky út
VI. Andrássy út 3
Tues–Sun 10 a.m.–5.30 p.m.

A museum devoted to the history of the Hungarian postal service might not in itself sound very enticing, but this one is not only surprisingly entertaining but also allows the chance to see inside one of Andrássy út's impressive mansions. The stairway and entrance are outstanding, with frescoes by Károly Lotz.

State Opera House

Magyar Állami Operaház D 4
M1 Opera
VI. Andrássy út 22
Guided tours daily, 3 and 4 p.m.

The wonderful neo-Renaissance Opera was designed by Miklós Ybl and built between 1875 and 1884. It's worth taking a tour of the building if you can't make it to a performance. Mahler and Klemperer conducted here, Liszt composed music for its opening. With its dazzling main staircase, frescoed auditorium and brilliant ceiling painting by Károly Lotz, it represents the cultural highpoint of Budapest's Golden Age.

From Opera to Oktogon D 4

This section of Andrássy út has the best of the district's entertainment and nightlife. Opposite the Opera on Dalszínház utca, take a look at the striking Art Nouveau **Új Színház** theatre, built in 1910 as the Parisiana nightclub. A block up from the Opera, Nagymező utca has a couple of theatres that put on blockbuster musicals, and several late-night bars and clubs. Liszt Ferenc tér, just before Oktogon, boasts some of the city's trendiest cafés, a market and the splendid Art Nouveau **Academy of Music**, with regular classical music concerts.

House of Terror

- Terror Háza Múzeum E 4
- M1 Oktogon
- VI. Andrássy út 60
- Tues–Fri 10 a.m.–6 p.m.,
- Sat, Sun 10 a.m.–7.30 p.m.

In 1944 this was the seat of the Hungarian National Socialist Party. From 1945 to 1956 the Communist secret services used the rooms for interrogations, torture and executions. The building was converted into a memorial in 2001–02. A permanent multi-media exhibition reveals the methods of the two 20th-century reigns of terror.

Franz Liszt Museum

- Liszt Ferenc Emlékmúzeum E 4
- M1 Vörösmarty utca
- VI. Vörösmarty utca 35
- Mon–Fri 10 a.m.–6 p.m.,
- Sat 9 a.m.–5 p.m.

Turn right off Andrássy út onto Vörösmarty utca, where you will immediately find the house where Franz Liszt (1811–86) lived for the last seven years of his life. The three rooms of his upstairs apartment contain photos, letters and music scores. There's also Liszt's Broadwood piano, once owned by Beethoven, and his ingenious composing desk with a built-in mini keyboard. Recitals are often held on Saturday mornings.

Kodály Memorial Museum

- Kodály Emlékmúzeum E 3
- M1 Kodály körönd
- VI. Kodály körönd 1
- Wed 10 a.m.–4 p.m.,
- Thu–Sat 10 a.m.–6 p.m.,
- Sun 10 a.m.–2 p.m.

Along with Liszt and Bartók, Zoltán Kodály (1882–1967) completes Hungary's triumvirate of great composers. Here in his house you can see his book-lined study, piano, manuscripts and a collection of jugs which, like his music, typify his love of traditional Hungarian folk art.

Ferenc Hopp Museum of Asiatic Art

- Hopp Ferenc Kelet-Àsziai Művészeti Múzeum
- M1 Bajza utca
- VI. Andrássy út 103
- Tues–Sun 10 a.m.–6 p.m.

Wealthy businessman Ferenc Hopp amassed an impressive collection of Eastern art—including Chinese Buddhist sculptures, Indian paintings and Japanese silks.

György Ráth Museum

- M1 Bajza utca
- Trolleybus 70, 78
- VI. Városligeti fasor 12
- Tues–Sun 10 a.m.–6 p.m.

Turn right onto Bajza utca, just before the Ferenc Hopp Museum, and walk a couple of blocks to a

Andrássy út and City Park

City Park packs culture, leisure and entertainment into the former royal hunting ground.

beautiful collection of oriental arts and crafts. Decorative Japanese combs, Samurai armour, Utagawa wood-block prints, Chinese vases, scrolls and silk-paintings can all be admired in the elegant Art Nouveau house of art historian György Ráth.

Heroes' Square

M1 Hősök tere
XIV. Hősök tere

Andrássy út ends at this grandiose testament to Hungarian nationalism. It was laid out for the 1896 celebrations. At the centre of the square, the 36-m-high (118-ft) **Millenary Monument** is topped by a statue of the Archangel Gabriel who, legend has it, prompted the Pope's offer of the Hungarian crown to King Stephen. At its base are Árpád and the Magyar chiefs, and in the colonnades behind are statues of national heroes from Stephen to Lajos Kossuth, leader of the 1848 Revolution.

The square is flanked by two huge neoclassical buildings. On the south side, the **Műcsarnok gallery** dates from 1895 and puts on temporary exhibitions of Hungarian and foreign artists. Opposite is the Museum of Fine Arts.

Museum of Fine Arts
Szépművészeti Múzeum
M1 Hősök tere
XIV. Hősök tere
Daily (except Mon)
10 a.m.–5.30 p.m.

One of Europe's finest collections of art, with Egyptian, Greek and Roman relics thrown in for good measure. From Italian Renaissance to French Impressionism, all the big names are here—Leonardo and Raphael, Titian, Dürer, Rubens, Cézanne, Monet and Renoir. The Spanish art is outstanding, with works by Goya, Velázquez and Murillo, and the most significant group of paintings by El Greco outside Spain.

City Park
Városliget
M1 Hősök tere
XIV. Városliget
Museum open Tues–Fri, Sun
10 a.m. –5 p.m., Sat to 6 p.m.

Budapest's main park attained its present size and layout as the site of the 1896 Millenary Exhibition. Near the entrance is an attractive lake, where you can go boating in summer or ice skating in winter beneath the turrets of Vajdahunyad Castle. Built specifically to provide an appropriately Hungarian backdrop to the exhibition, the castle is modelled on Vajdahunyad

in Transylvania. It now houses the **Agriculture Museum** (Mezőgazdasági Múzeum), which looks at Hungarian farming through the ages. Near the castle is a mock-Romanesque Catholic church, and further along, the statue of a hooded figure entitled "Anonymous", honouring the unnamed medieval chronicler without whom the nation's history would have remained in the dark.

Petőfi Hall
Petőfi Csarnok
M1 Mexikói út
Trolleybus 72,74
XIV. Városliget
Apr–Oct Tues–Sun 10 a.m.–6 p.m.

A short distance east of the castle complex is Petőfi Hall. There's a Museum of Aviation and Space Travel on the second floor, while the main arena is given over to rock concerts and occasional discos. They even manage to pack in a weekend **flea market** here as well (closes at 1 p.m.).

Transport Museum
Közlekedési Múzeum
M1 Mexikói út/Trolleybus 72, 74
XIV. Városligeti körút 11
Tues–Fri 10 a.m.–4 p.m., Sat and Sun 10 a.m.–5 p.m.

Outside this museum, in the eastern corner of the park, you can see the remnants of Budapest's Danube bridges, all of which were blown up during World War II. The museum displays old trains, automobiles and trams, and there's a model railway with engines chugging around a miniature Hungary.

Széchenyi Baths

- M1 Széchenyi fürdő
- XIV. Állatkerti körút 11
- Open daily in summer
- 6 a.m.–7 p.m.,
- in winter Mon–Fri 6 a.m.–6 p.m.

The splendid neo-baroque bathhouse was completed in 1913. Its thermal waters well up from almost a kilometre below the surface, and at 27°C provide year-round open-air bathing. Mixed bathing is allowed here but it's better known for attracting aquatic chess-players with floating chessboards.

Vidám Park

- M1 Széchenyi fürdő
- XIV. Állatkerti körút 14–16
- In summer Tues–Sun
- 9.45 a.m.–8 p.m.,
- winter 9.45 a.m.–sunset

Old-fashioned amusement park entertainment, such as dodgems, a ferris wheel, merry-go-round and other rides to keep adrenalin levels well under control.

Circus

- M1 Széchenyi fürdő
- XIV. Állatkerti körút 7
- Performances Mon–Fri 3 p.m.,
- 7 p.m., Sat, Sun 10.30 a.m.,
- 3 p.m., 7 p.m.

Performances by Hungarian and international troupes.

Zoo

- M1 Széchenyi fürdő
- XIV. Állatkerti körút 6–12
- In summer Tues–Sun 9 a.m.–
- / p.m., winter 9 a.m.–4 p.m.

Animals big and small live beyond the superb Art Nouveau entrance—an Indian elephant base and polar bear canopy. The Palm House was built by Eiffel, of tower fame, and the Elephant House is amazing.

Hungarian Historical Railway Park

- Magyar Vasúttörténeti Park
- Bus 30 from Keleti pályaudvar railway station to Rokolya utca stop, or special "Ingajárat" train from Nyugati pálaudvar railway station at 9.45 and every hour until 4.45
- XIV. Tatai út 95
- Apr–Oct 10 a.m.–6 p.m.;
- Nov–Mar 10 a.m.–3 p.m.

Pretty park with restored steam and diesel engines, Europe's biggest functioning turntable, restaurants, souvenir shop.

EXCURSIONS

Picturesque historic towns, the famous Danube Bend, the Puszta with its splendid horses, and one of the biggest lakes in Europe all lie within easy reach of Budapest. You can get to them quickly by car or train. More pleasurable, though certainly slower, is a cruise along the Danube, the perfect way to find a cool breeze on a steamy summer's day.

THE DANUBE BEND

Just north of Budapest, Europe's great east-flowing artery (the Hungarians call it the Duna) dramatically changes direction, plunging south en route to the Black Sea. The Danube Bend *(Dunakanyar)*, a name that covers the whole region as well as this geographical phenomenon, is one of the most spectacular points along the river's entire 2,850 km (1,770 miles). What's more, you can also visit delightful old cities such as the baroque Szentendre or the once-powerful Esztergom and Visegrád. These were Hungary's medieval royal seat and capital, before the Mongol invasion forced the move to Buda. Esztergom remains the nation's ecclesiastical centre to this day.

Szentendre

HÉV train from Batthyány tér or summer boat service from Vigadó tér.

20 km (12 miles) north of Budapest

Szentendre (St Andrew) is a photogenic little town, with cobblestone streets, old churches and a surprising quantity of art galleries and museums. Founded by Serbian refugees fleeing the Turks after the Battle of Kosovo in 1389, it received a second wave of Serbs three centuries later when the Turks recaptured Belgrade. Early in the 20th century, the town became something of an artists' colony, which explains the number of galleries.

The centre of town is the baroque **Fő tér**, with a votive cross put up by Serbian merchants in 1763 to celebrate the non-appearance of the plague. Here, too, is the green-spired Greek Orthodox **Blagoveštenska Church**, built ten years earlier. The icons inside are emphatically Serbian, however, and evoke the troubled history of that land. Next to the church, in an 18th-century schoolhouse, the **Ferenczy Museum** is devoted to

Stuccoed baroque houses surround Szentendre's pretty main square.

the family who pioneered the artists' colony. Here you'll find Károly Ferenczy's Impressionist work alongside paintings and sculptures by his sons. On the south side of Fő tér, the **Kmetty Museum** houses dark, disturbing canvases by the Cubist János Kmetty, who moved to Szentendre in 1930.

Just behind the square's east side, an alley leads to the **Margit Kovács Museum**. Kovács, who died in 1977, created stylized, elongated sculptures from ceramics, and her work—part reinvention of religious iconic art, part folksy kitsch—is both striking and entertaining.

The **Templomdomb** (Church Hill) sits above Fő tér, and has a splendid view of the town. The Catholic **Parish Church** here was begun in the 13th century, though what you see today is largely a baroque reconstruction. In the summer, lively weekend craft fairs are held on the square outside the church.

Opposite, at the **Czóbel Museum**, bold brushwork and a passion for colour are on display in the work of Fauvist artist Béla Czóbel.

There's more evidence of Szentendre's Serbian connection a little to the north. With its dark red spire, the stunning **Belgrade Church** is unmistakable. Dating from the 1760s, it's undoubtedly the finest Serbian Orthodox church in town. Nearby, the **Serbian Ecclesiastical Art Collection** contains the church's superb icons, religious artworks and vestments. Leading south from Fő tér, Dumtsa Jenő utca has two excellent, if contrasting, museums. The **Barcsay Museum** has architectural paintings, mosaics and tapestries by Transylvanian artist Jenő Barcsay. An altogether lighter confection can be enjoyed at the **Marzipan Museum**, where those with a sweet tooth can lick their lips over such items as a marzipan sculpture of the Parliament.

Away from the centre, but well worth seeking out, the **Open Air Village Museum** has traditional rural houses, churches and farm buildings, brought from around the Hungarian countryside and reassembled here. Get there by bus 8, but bear in mind that it's only open from April to October.

Visegrád

Commanding the river bend, Visegrád—High Castle—was both a medieval hilltop fortress and royal capital of Hungary. Its early history mirrors that of Buda: the citadel was built by Béla IV after the Mongol invasion, and the palace by the 14th-century Angevin kings. It reached its cultural zenith under King Matthias and was then left to crumble by the Turks. But that's where the similarity ends. Visegrád was buried under a mudslide and remained lost until the 1930s, when excavation began.

The partly reconstructed **Royal Palace** is at the foot of Visegrád's steep hill. Founded by King Charles Robert, it was the setting for the 1335 Visegrád Congress, attended by the Hungarian, Polish and Czech monarchs to discuss the growing Habsburg threat. In the next century, Vlad the Impaler, the prototype for Dracula, was held prisoner here.

There's not a lot left of the old palace. The Court of Honour, however, has a fine Renaissance loggia and the red marble Hercules Fountain. Elsewhere, the Lion Fountain is a replica of Matthias's original, with his raven crest and lots of lions. The remains of the original fountains, along with other excavated finds from the palace, can be seen in a museum inside the hexagonal **Solomon's Tower**, further up the hill.

It's an exacting 25-minute hike up the icon-lined Path of Calvary to the once-mighty **Citadel** (though you can also take a bus from near the Mahart riverboat pier). Needless to say, the views are spectacular, although if they leave you wanting even more, you can make your way across the wooded hills to the 377-m (1,237-ft) **Nagyvillám Lookout Tower**, with vistas extending all the way to Slovakia.

Esztergom

A scenic 20-km (12-mile) boat ride west from Visegrád brings you to Hungary's first capital and royal seat under the Árpád kings. King

---

GOING FOR THE JUGULAR

Belief in vampires was widespread in Hungary until relatively recently, but it was the life of Transylvanian terror Vlad the Impaler that mainly inspired books such as *Dracula*. His charming nickname arose from his taste for decapitating enemies and impaling their heads on poles with which he would later decorate his castle. Though the castle is in modern Romania, when Vlad was busy being bloodthirsty back in the 15th century, Transylvania was part of Hungary, and his transgressions eventually landed him under King Matthias's lock and key in Visegrád from 1462 to 1475. All the more appropriate, therefore, that when the classic film of *Dracula* became a hit in Hollywood in the 1930s, the vampire should have been played by Hungarian-born Béla Lugosi.

The warm waters of Hévíz, just west of Lake Balaton, are renowned for their therapeutic properties.

Stephen was born here around 970, and founded the cathedral in 1010. The monarchy moved out after the Mongol invasions of the 13th century, but the archbishops stayed on, taking over the royal residence as their own. Esztergom was to pay the price for its ecclesiastical importance in 1543, when it was destroyed by the Turks. The restoration needed was so considerable that the Church only moved back again in 1820. And despite its clergy facing brutal persecution by the Communist authorities in the 1950s and 60s, the city has remained the centre of Hungarian Catholicism throughout. The gigantic neoclassical **Basilica** that towers over the city skyline today is on the site of King Stephen's original cathedral. Begun in 1822, it took nearly 40 years to complete. The massive dome is based on St Peter's in Rome, and when it was finished, a consecration ceremony was held to the accompaniment of Liszt's specially composed *Gran Mass* ("Gran" being the German name for Esztergom).

The most outstanding feature of the voluminous interior is the **Bakócz Chapel**, built in red marble by Florentine Renaissance craftsmen in the early 16th century. Resurrected from the ruins, it's the only part of the old cathedral left. To the right of the main altar, the **treasury** contains a magnificent collection of textiles and medieval gold relics, including the 13th-century Coronation Cross, used by Hungary's kings to pledge their oaths up to the last coronation—of Charles IV—in 1916. In the **crypt** is the tomb of Cardinal Mindszenty. The Cardinal opposed the Communist takeover after the war and was arrested and tortured. Released during the 1956 Uprising, he took refuge in the US Embassy for the next 15 years. He died in exile in 1975 and was reburied here with a state funeral in 1991. You can complete your tour of the church by ascending the **cupola** for a superb view of both town and river. You'll need plenty of energy to tackle the last stage: a narrow, interminable spiral staircase, but it's well worth the effort.

Next to the cathedral, the **Castle Museum** incorporates parts of the royal palace, including a 12th-century chapel and medieval Hall of Virtues, named after the frescoes depicting Moderation, Justice, Fortitude and Prudence. Below the hill are the attractive baroque streets of the **Víziváros**, or Watertown. The **Parish Church** dates from 1738 and is in Italianate baroque style. Nearby, in the old Primate's Palace, the **Christian Museum** houses what ranks as Hungary's greatest collection of religious art, with Italian prints, Renaissance paintings and the ornate 15th-century Garamszentbenedek coffin, once used in Easter Week processions.

Lake Balaton

Landlocked Central Europeans have long treated the lake as an alternative seaside. The Romans built villas here, the Magyars liked it for the fishing (it supports 40 different species, including the famous *fogas,* or pike-perch), the opening of the railway line in the 1860s brought in floods of tourists, and during the Communist era, East Germans were allowed to holiday along its shores and meet up with their rich friends and relations from West Germany. With the collapse of the Berlin Wall, hotels are finding life tougher, and even the three-star establishments are looking slightly the worse for wear, but the area is still immensely popular with Germans, Austrians, Swiss Germans and, of course, Hungarians themselves.

There are plenty of rooms to rent—

just look for the "Zimmer frei" signs. Balaton is one of the largest lakes in Europe. It is strikingly elongated, stretching for 77 km (48 miles) along the foothills of the Bakony Mountains, but only 14 km (8.7 miles) across at its widest point. It is also remarkably shallow—a mere 11 m (36 ft) at its maximum depth. This has some interesting side effects. It freezes over completely in winter, making it one of the world's great skating rinks, while in summer the water heats up like a thermal bath. Its shallowness also makes it vulnerable to strong winds, which can create high waves in a matter of minutes.

The lakewater is packed with minerals which, given the Hungarian love of spas, means there are a number of health resorts. **Balatonfüred**, on the northeast shore, has been frequented for its medicinal springs for the last 250 years. On **Gyógy tér**, the charming baroque main square, you can sample thermal mineral water from the Kossuth Well. Down near the Balaton ferry pier is a bust of the Indian poet Rabindranath Tagore, who convalesced in the town and wrote a poem about it that's reproduced on a plaque here. Visible to the west is the beautiful **Tihany peninsula**, which almost cuts the lake in half. The peninsula is now a protected National Park, and a good place for hiking, with plenty of fine lake views to be had. The town of **Tihany** occupies a hill overlooking a small inner lake. In the centre of town, the **Abbey Church** is one of Hungary's most splendid baroque monuments. Dating from 1754, it has magnificent twin towers, while inside are fine baroque altars, pulpit and organ. More important still is the 11th-century crypt containing the tomb of King Andrew I, who founded the original abbey on this site in 1055.

The **Abbey Museum** next door is in a converted 18th-century monastery, and has informative displays on the lake and some Roman remains in the basement. Not far from the church, a small **open-air museum** preserves old houses from Balaton's traditional fishing communities. Continue along the promenade to Echo Hill, with superb views and, if you shout loud enough, the chance to enjoy the sound of your own voice.

Some 25 km (16 miles) further west is **Badacsony**, whose rich soil and benevolent climate make it one of Hungary's top wine-producing regions. Vineyards cling to the conical Mt Badacsony, an extinct volcano, while in the foothills just above the town there's an interesting wine museum. Tastings take place in the cellar, and outside there's a fantastic view of the lake. You can reach the museum from town by taking an open-topped jeep—they go from outside the post office. First, though, check out the **József Egry Museum**. This displays paintings by the eponymous Egry (1883–1951), one of Balaton's most notable artists.

At the lake's western tip, **Keszthely** was once the playground of the Festetics, an aristocratic family who owned the entire area in the 18th century. Their stunning baroque palace now houses the **Helikon Castle Museum**. Visitors can only see one wing of the vast building, but that includes the 90,000-volume Helikon Library, a collection of ancient weapons, and rooms rich with art and period furniture.

One of the illustrious Festetics, Count György, founded Europe's first school of agriculture here in 1797, and its descendant, a large agricultural university, gives the town a lively student scene that makes it unlike any of the lake's other tourist resorts. The Count is understandably a revered figure these days, and the **Georgikon Farm Museum**, on the site of the original school, is devoted both to him and to the farming techniques of his time.

South from the centre, you can see old photos of the lake and learn about its history at the **Balaton Museum**.

The lake's southern shore is noticeably brasher, and a more hedonistic culture rules within its heavily built-up resorts. For a taste of just how hedonistic, head for **Siófok** on the southeast shore. Catering to a large German and Austrian clientele, the town's hotels stretch for 15 km (9 miles) along the waterfront. In the centre, the Strand throngs with sun-seekers by day; by night, the town buzzes with tourists flowing between bars, restaurants, beer gardens and nightclubs.

North of the lake at Herend, visit the **Porcelanium**: a modern complex near the factory comprising a "Minimanufacture", museum, shop and the Apicius restaurant, where each table is set with a different hand-painted Herend service. It is open in summer daily 9 a.m.–4.30 p.m.; in winter Tues–Sat 9 a.m.–3.30 p.m. The guided tour begins with a short film, then you can watch all the different stages of production, from rolling out the raw "dough" like pastry to painting the last

exquisite leaves and petals. Book in advance:
tel. (0036) 88 523 190
fax (0036) 88 261 518
Web site: www.porcelanium.com

Puszta

Also known as the Great Plain (*Nagyalföld*), this vast, flat prairie was Hungary's very own Wild West during the 19th century, when huge herds of cattle grazed here watched over by rough-and-tough cowboys, called *gulyás*. It seems an unchanging landscape, but the popular name, Puszta, meaning "bleak" or "abandoned", tells a different story. It's hard to believe now, but it was once covered in thick forest. It was laid waste during the Turkish occupation, because of the invaders' need for timber to build fortresses, and became a virtual desert. Its renaissance as pastureland was due to the irrigation works on the River Tisza employed by Count Széchenyi in the early 19th century. But by the 20th century, the success of the irrigation scheme meant it could sustain crop development, and big landowners carried out wholesale enclosure, killing off the cattle industry and creating widespread poverty among the peasants. Yet more changes were in the offing. Under post-war communism, the estates were nationalized, and huge collective farms introduced, only to be broken up after 1989 and returned to private ownership. Today, visitors will find pleasant little towns—**Kecskemét** and **Szeged** in particular are worth spending time in—beyond which are attractive old whitewashed farmsteads adorned with bright-coloured strings of paprika. The plains, meanwhile, are as strong on atmosphere as ever.

Southwest of Kecskemét, the **Kiskunság National Park** offers in concentrated form a true taste of the Puszta, with plenty of great hiking and cycling trails. Probably the most enjoyable way of seeing the place is on horseback. Horse-riding trips can be arranged in Kecskemét, as well as through tour operators in Budapest.

The cowboy past lives on at **Bugac**, on the edge of the national park. Here, you can take a horse-drawn carriage to the **Herder Museum**, where the plains' exotic flora and fauna (albeit stuffed) are displayed, and then enjoy a Hungarian rodeo with plenty of trick horse-riding.

Riders in the puszta demonstrate their skills on teams of five horses.

Dining Out

Whereas Budapest's grand Habsburg-era coffee houses seem to defy time, its restaurant scene has moved at an incredible pace since the late 1980s, with new places coming and going with amazing frequency. This chapter has selected those most likely to stay the distance, and there's a marvellous range to choose from. You will find in them all manner of delicious international and Hungarian fare, from world-famous goulash and Bull's Blood wine to mouth-watering dishes based on favourite Hungarian ingredients.

Restaurants are uniformly good value. The following recommendations are marked with the $$$ price symbol to give some idea of what you might expect to pay per head for a three-course meal excluding wine. $ is budget price, $$ is around 2,000–4,000 Ft and $$$ is upwards of 4,000 Ft.

CASTLE HILL

Alabárdos
Shuttle bus from M2 Moszkva tér
I. Országház utca 2
Tel. 356 0851
Mon–Sat noon–4 p.m.
and 7 p.m.–11 p.m.
This delightful 15th-century mansion close to the Matthias church is home to Hungarian, international and Transylvanian cuisine. Live guitar music. $$$

Aranyhordó
Shuttle bus from M2 Moszkva tér
I. Tárnok utca 16
Tel. 356 1367
Open daily noon–midnight
Adorned with frescoes, crossbows and battleaxes, the restaurant makes the most of its 14th-century location. It specializes in fish dishes—try the roast buttered *fogas* with dill and crayfish ragout for a mouthwatering treat. $$$

Café Miró
Shuttle bus from M2 Moszkva tér
I. Úri utca 30
Tel. 375 5458
Open daily 9 a.m.–midnight
The trendiest spot in Castle Hill to relax with cake and coffee. Its inspiration is the work of surrealist Spanish artist Joán Miró, and with furniture to match it's like sitting inside one of his paintings. $$

Pierrot
- Shuttle bus from M2 Moszkva tér
- I. Fortuna utca 14
- Tel. 375 6971
- Open daily 11 a.m.–1 a.m.

A good alternative to the establishments at the more touristy end of Castle Hill, the Pierrot has the honour of being Budapest's first post-communist privately run café-restaurant. It has a solid selection of Hungarian and international cooking, but specializes in crêpes. $$

Ruszwurm Cukrászda
- Shuttle bus from M2 Moszkva tér
- I. Szentháromság utca 7
- Tel. 375 5284
- Open daily 10 a.m.–7 p.m.

Founded in the 1820s, and still with some of its original cherrywood interior, this little café serves coffee, cakes and ices in what looks like somebody's cosy front parlour. $–$$

BUDA

Angelika
- M2 Batthyány tér
- I. Batthyány tér 7
- Tel. 212 3784
- Open daily 10 a.m.–10 p.m.

In the former presbytery of beautiful St Anne's Church, and with 18th-century vaulted ceilings and stained-glass windows, Angelika is an oasis of calm. Take time out from the hurly-burly of the Buda riverside to enjoy a good selection of coffee and cakes. $–$$

Arany Kaviár
- M2 Moszkva tér
- I. Ostrom utca 19
- Tel. 201 6737
- Open daily 4 p.m.–midnight

Quality Russian cuisine with such fare as blinis, Tsar-style salmon, Beluga caviar and, of course, a wide range of vodkas. $$$

Café Gusto
- Tram 4, 6
- II. Frankel Leó út 12
- Tel. 316 3970
- Mon–Sat 10 a.m.–10 p.m.

A small Italian-influenced café with fine seafood and salads. Also good for coffee and desserts. $$

Marxim's
- Tram 4, 6
- II. Kisrókus utca 23
- Tel. 316 0231/315 0750
- Mon–Thurs noon–1 a.m.,
- Fri and Sat noon–2 a.m.,
- Sun 6 p.m.–1 a.m.

Long live the Revolution! Well, it lives on here in Marxim's Gulag and KGB pizzas and Lenin salad at least. Popular with locals, who occupy booths separated by barbed-wire. $

Szent Jupát

- M2 Moszkva tér
- II. Retek utca 16
- Tel. 212 2923
- Open noon–6 a.m.

A cosy and friendly restaurant serving Hungarian cuisine in satisfying portions. A favourite with young people: excellent value for money. $

Vadrózsa

- Bus 11, 91
- II. Pentelei Molnár utca 15
- Tel. 326 5817
- Open daily noon–3 p.m.
- and 7 p.m.–midnight

Fine traditional Hungarian cuisine such as goulash, paprika chicken and stuffed peppers, in a beautiful baroque villa on the Rózsadomb. $$$

ÓBUDA

Kéhli

- HÉV Árpád híd/Tram 1
- III. Mókus utca 22
- Tel. 368 0613
- Daily noon–midnight

When it was founded a hundred years ago, Kéhli was in bucolic surroundings—now it nestles among concrete tower blocks. The good news is, it retains an attractive rustic decor and peasant-sized portions of what many consider the best Hungarian cooking in town. $$

Kisbuda Gyöngye

- Tram 17
- III. Kenyeres utca 34
- Tel. 368 6402
- Open daily noon–midnight

SOME LIKE IT RED

It's not known for sure how paprika made its way to Hungary from its point of origin in the Americas, but this pungent spice has become the quintessential flavour—and colour—of Hungarian cuisine since it first appeared here in the 17th century. It is made from the glossy red capsicum pod, dried and ground into a peppery powder. It's grown in vast quantities around the Great Plains, and the Hungarian strain is generally agreed to be the finest variety in the world. Not only that, paprika is richer in vitamin C than citrus fruit—it's no accident that the man who received the Nobel Prize for first synthesizing vitamin C was Albert Szent-Györgyi of Szeged University, which lies at the centre of Hungary's paprika-growing region. As you treat your taste buds to a plate of rich and spicy goulash, you can savour the thought that you're getting a healthy dose of vitamins at the same time.

Fin-de-siècle-style salon, interesting specialities and very popular with locals. $$

MARGARET ISLAND

Széchenyi
Bus 26
XIII. Danubius Grand Hotel,
Margaret Island
Tel. 889 4700
Open daily noon–3 p.m.
and 7 p.m.–11 p.m.
Situated in a stately old hotel, the restaurant has good Transylvanian-style cuisine, a gypsy band in the evening and a huge summer terrace overlooking the park. $$–$$$

BELVÁROS

Apostolok
M3 Ferenciek tere
V. Kígyó utca 4–6
Tel. 318 3559
Open daily noon–midnight
Proclaiming itself the only restaurant in Budapest with a neo-Gothic interior, the Apostolok is high on atmosphere and strong on traditional pork dishes. $$

Carmel Pince
M2 Astoria
VII. Kazinczy utca 31
Tel. 322 1834
Open daily noon–11 p.m.

Old-style cellar restaurant in the Jewish quarter. It's especially strong on goose, an important feature of Hungarian Jewish cuisine. $$

Cyrano
- M1 Vörösmarty tér
- V. Kristóf tér 7–8
- Tel. 266 3096
- Open daily 11 a.m.–5 p.m. and 6.30 p.m.–midnight

Delicious French-oriented cuisine in a delightful setting. Try cream-covered peaches stuffed with Roquefort and move on to steak and goose liver, but remember to wear something with an expandable waistline. $$–$$$

Fatál
- M3 Kálvin tér/Tram 2
- V. Váci utca 67 (entrance in Pintér utca)
- Tel. 266 2607
- Open daily 11.30 a.m.–2 a.m.
- Booking essential

The name means nothing more deadly than "wooden plate", though the vast size of the portions you'll get on it may have you worried. This is one of Budapest's most touristy restaurants, and the service is sometimes surly. $

Gerbeaud
- M1 Vörösmarty tér
- V. Vörösmarty tér 7
- Tel. 429 9000
- Open daily 9 a.m.–9 p.m.; June–Sept to 10.30 p.m.

A relic of the Habsburg era, this sumptuous Art Nouveau café became famous around 1900 under Emil Gerbeaud. Born in Geneva into a family of confectioners, he was an artist in chocolate and chestnut cream, and his recipes retain their powerful hold on any self-respecting cake-lover's imagination. The service is brusque and the clientele mainly tourists—but what does that matter when you're tucking into a slice of their special six-layered caramel-topped Dobos cake surrounded by such delightfully decadent splendour. $$

Irene Légrády Antique
- M1, M2, M3 Deák tér
- V. Bárczy István utca 3–5
- Tel. 266 4993
- Mon–Fri noon–3 p.m., 7 p.m.–midnight; Sat 7 p.m.–midnight

Tucked away on the first floor of a small antique shop, this discreet, stylish restaurant is itself furnished with antiques. The game and fish dishes are particularly good, and there's gypsy music performed in the evenings. $$$

Kárpátia
- M3 Ferenciek tere
- V. Ferenciek tere 7–8

- Tel. 317 3596
- Open daily 11 a.m.–11 p.m.

Splendid turn-of-the-century interior, traditional Hungarian cuisine and live gypsy music make this central restaurant well worth checking out. $$

Légrádi & Társa
- M3 Kálvin tér
- V. Magyar utca 23
- Tel. 318 6804
- Mon–Sat 6 p.m.–midnight

Intimate, traditional and upmarket, Légrádi's combines drawing-room elegance with exceptionally tasty food. Booking is advisable. $$$

Múzeum
- M3 Kálvin tér
- VIII. Múzeum körút 12
- Tel. 267 0375
- Mon–Sat 10.30 a.m.–1.30 a.m.

If walking around the National Museum has worked up your appetite, this superb restaurant is just next door. Its frescoed interior exemplifies 19th-century elegance, and the well-presented Hungarian and international cuisine is first-class. $$–$$$

Resti Kocsma
- M1 Vörösmarty tér
- V. Deák Ferenc utca 2
- Tel. 266 6210
- Mon–Sat noon–5 a.m.

Communist-era memorabilia, red-checked tablecloths and a large menu offering all manner of flesh and fowl. The décor is fraying at the edges, but a band plays old Hungarian tunes. $–$$

Százéves
- M3 Ferenciek tere/Tram 2
- V. Pesti Barnabás utca 2
- Tel. 318 3608
- Open daily noon–midnight

Located in a baroque house dating from the 1750s, the restaurant itself was founded in 1831. There's an extensive menu, which includes some excellent venison dishes, and a large cellar of both Hungarian and international wines. $$–$$$

LIPÓTVÁROS

Biarritz
- Tram 2 Kossuth Lajos tér
- V. Balassi Bálint utca 2
- Tel. 311 4413
- Mon–Fri 9 a.m.–midnight; Sat, Sun 10 a.m.–midnight

Sit cheek by jowl with the nation's politicos from the Parliament and graze on good salads or gorge on lamb and poultry dishes. $$

Café Kör
- M3 Arany János utca
- V. Sas utca 17

Tel. 311 0053
Mon–Sat 10 a.m.–10 p.m.
Vibrant downtown bistro with inventive Hungarian menu and good wine list. Popular with locals and foreigners. $$

Iguana

M2 Kossuth tér
V. Zoltán utca 16
Tel. 331 4352
Mon–Sat 11.30 a.m.–00.30 a.m.
This is the place the expats come to party. Tex-Mex tacos and burritos are the order of the day, while the flowing margaritas and blasting music give it the air of a raucous holiday resort. $–$$

Lou Lou

M2 Kossuth tér or tram 2
V. Vigyázó Ferenc 4
Tel. 312 4505
Mon–Fri noon–3 p.m. and 7–11 p.m., Sat 7–11 p.m.
Booking essential
Top-notch French-Hungarian restaurant with only a handful of tables. Stylishly served fish, meat and game, superb sauces, dependable wine list. $$–$$$

Marquis de Salade

M3 Nyugati
VI. Hajós utca 43
Tel. 302 4086
Open daily noon–midnight
A rarity on two counts—a punning name that's amusing and a Budapest restaurant to keep vegetarians happy. There's a large selection of salads, together with intriguing non-vegetarian dishes from as far afield as Azerbaijan and China. $

Művészinas

M3 Deák tér
VI. Bajcsy-Zsilinszky út 9
Tel. 268 1439
Open daily noon–midnight
Classy and romantic restaurant with a 19th-century atmosphere. $$$

Szerb

M3 Nyugati
V. Nagy Ignác utca 16
Tel. 269 3139
Mon–Sat 11 a.m.–8 p.m.
A good place to start if you want a taste of Balkan cuisine. Dishes are definitely on the meaty side. Sample *duvec*, a meat-and-potato stew. $

Szindbád

M3 Nyugati
V. Markó utca 33
Tel. 332 2966
Mon–Sat noon–midnight
The emphasis is on excellent service at this attractive cellar-restaurant, beginning with an invitation to drinks at "the club", a bar area

where you can sink into the welcoming arms of a capacious Chesterfield. The Hungarian-international food is good, if on the conservative side, while the atmosphere is unashamedly old-fashioned. $$$

ANDRÁSSY ÚT & CITY PARK

Articsóka
- M1 Opera/M3 Arany János utca
- VI. Zichy Jenőutca 17
- Tel. 302 7757

- Open daily noon–midnight
- Booking advised

A palm-tree décor, a roof-terrace café and flavoursome mediterranean-style cuisine all add up to make this very much Budapest's current in-place, frequented by a fashionable crowd. $$

Bagolyvár
- M1 Hősök tere
- XIV. Állatkerti út 2
- Tel. 468 3110
- Open daily noon–11 p.m.

HUNGARIAN WINE

Hungary will keep the most demanding wine-lover in a state of bliss. It's a huge producer of quality wines, with the renowned Tokaji (also spelt Tokay) as the jewel in its crown. Made in the Tokaj region of the Northern Uplands, the wine uses native Furmint and Hárslevelü grapes and ranges from the dry Tokaji Furmint to the rich Tokaji aszú dessert wine. The latter is one of the world's great sweet wines and has had its praises sung by Louis XIV, Beethoven, Schubert and Robert Browning—even Sherlock Holmes is known to have had the odd glass. Its degree of sweetness is expressed in *puttonyos*, numbered from 3 to 6 (the sweetest) and indicating the quantity of baskets (*puttony*) of "noble" grapes added to each barrel of wine.

More popularly identified with Hungary is Bull's Blood from around Eger (Egri Bikavér), a red table wine whose name tells you all you need to know about its full-bodied character. This goes perfectly with Hungary's abundance of meaty dishes, as do the younger reds, Kékfrankos and Kékoportó, and the fine Villányi-Burgundi.

To accompany Lake Balaton fish, try a Lake Balaton wine. The Romans, who first brought wine-growing techniques to Hungary, loved the wines made here. From the vineyards around Badacsony, on the lake's north shore, look out for a range of white wines using well-known grape varieties, including the Olaszrízling, a medium-bodied Riesling, Traminer and Pinot Blanc.

Owned by Gundel next door, the Owl's Castle, as its name means, is less formal than its renowned neighbour and run exclusively by women. The excellent home-style Hungarian cuisine, aided by delicious soups and fresh-made bread, is great value. The interior is beautiful and the summer terrace overlooks the zoo. $$

Belcanto
- M1 Opera
- VI. Dalszínház utca 8
- Tel. 269 3101
- Open daily noon–3 p.m. and 6 p.m.–2 a.m.

If you can't get into the opera, try here—its neo-baroque design is almost as ornate as the real thing and the waiters are trained singers, who give a performance each evening at 8. The Italian food is good too. $$$

Biedermeier
- M1 Oktogon/Tram 4, 6
- VI. Moszár út 12
- Tel. 331 8942
- Open noon–3 p.m. and 6 p.m.–midnight

The furniture and music are 18th-century; the waiters are dressed in period costume; the atmosphere is cosy, candle-lit and intimate. As for the food, it's traditional Hungarian brought up to date. $$$

Café Mozart
- Tram 4, 6
- VII. Erzsébet körút 36
- Tel. 352 0664
- Mon–Fri, Sun 9 a.m.–11 p.m., Sat 9 a.m.–midnight

Mozart memorabilia and music abound and the waitresses wear daft period costumes, whereas the lighting is glitzily late 20th century. It's all very kitsch, but with more than 60 different types of coffee on the menu and a large no-smoking area, it has its good points. $–$$

Café Vian
- M1 Oktogon
- VI. Liszt Ferenc tér 9
- Tel. 268 1154
- Open daily 10 a.m.–midnight

Tasty sandwiches and salads along with an arty crowd. Seating on the square in summer makes it a good place for people-watching. $–$$

Hades Jazztaurant
- M1 Oktogon
- VI. Vörösmarty utca 31
- Tel. 3352 1503
- Mon–Fri noon–midnight; Sat 5 p.m.–midnight

Small jazzy restaurant decorated with characters of Greek mythology. Generous portions, very reasonable prices. Try the *pipi melle ahogy a szatir szereti*—chicken breast, satyr style. $

Gundel

- M1 Hősök tere
- XIV. Állakerti út 2
- Tel. 321 3550
- Open daily noon–4 p.m. and
- 6.30 p.m.–midnight

Budapest's most famous restaurant was founded in 1894 next to the city zoo. It was nationalized in 1949 and became a "collectivized catering unit", albeit retaining its reputation in gourmet circles. In 1991, Ronald S. Lauder and Hungarian-born restaurateur George Lang bought the establishment and restored it completely from ballroom to cellar. Today Gundel serves a light version of traditional cuisine in an elegant Art Nouveau setting, specializing in top-notch steaks, *fogas* (pike-perch) and sumptuous desserts such as the Gundel pancake, filled with nuts and raisins and covered in a chocolate and rum sauce. Booking is essential and, this being the last bastion of a bygone age, men are required to wear jacket and tie (unless you choose to dine in the garden). $$$

Lukács

- M1 Vörösmarty utca
- VI. Andrássy út 70
- Tel. 302 8747
- Mon–Fri 9 a.m.–8 p.m.,
- Sat and Sun 10 a.m.–8 p.m.

Frequented by members of the ÁVO secret police under the Communist regime—their HQ was at No. 60—Lukács now shares its premises with a bank, which slightly undermines its marble-and-chandelier pretensions to Grand Café status. Live piano music at tea time. $–$$

Művész

- M1 Opera
- VI. Andrássy út 29
- Tel. 352 1337
- Open daily 9 a.m.–10 p.m.

A great pre-opera spot, whose Golden Age gilt, huge mirrors and fin-de-siècle ambience give a foretaste of the Opera House itself. There's a decent selection of cakes, savouries and ices as long as you can engage the attention of the notoriously blasé waitresses. $–$$

Robinson

- M1 Hősök tere
- XIV. Városliget
- Tel. 422 0222
- Open daily noon–4 p.m.
- and 6 p.m.–midnight

Nicely situated on an island in the City Park lake. The extensive range of Hungarian and international dishes should make any budding Crusoes happy to be stranded here for a while. $$$

Entertainment

True to its cultural roots as a great central European capital and cultural melting pot, Budapest is a city that palpably buzzes with artistic vitality. Certainly, the Buda Hills—and the Pesti plains—are alive with the sound of music.

Details of what's on from day to day, be it music, film or festival, can be found in newspapers and listings magazines such as *The Budapest Sun*, *Scene* and *Pesti Est*.

MAJOR ARTS VENUES

Classical music is performed all year long in the great concert halls and opera houses, as well as in the big churches such as Matthias Church and St Stephen's Basilica. The Budapest Spring Festival, held in March, brings together the best in Hungarian art and music for a fortnight's cultural extravaganza.

At the major concert halls, performances are rarely sold out, and tickets are great value. They can be bought at the individual venue box office, or the Vigadó Ticket Service, Vörösmarty tér 1, tel. 327 4322 and Központi Jegyiroda, Andrássy út 15, tel. 267 9737.

Academy of Music
- Zeneakadémia E 4
- M1 Oktogon
- VI. Liszt Ferenc tér 8
- Tel. 342 0179

The Liszt Academy is based in a stunning Art Nouveau building.

Orchestral concerts and chamber recitals take place in the main hall.

Erkel Színház (off map)
- M2 Blaha Lujza tér
- VIII. Köztársaság tér 30
- Tel. 333 0540

Imaginatively-staged opera and ballet productions in cavernous communist-era theatre.

Merlin Theatre D 6
- M1, M2, M3 Deák tér
- V. Gerlóczy utca 4
- Tel. 317 9398

The best (and usually only) place to see English-language theatre in Budapest.

State Opera House
- Magyar Állami Operaház D 4
- M1 Opera
- VI. Andrássy út 22
- Tel. 353 0170

The opulent, frescoed interior of the magnificent State Opera House is the perfect setting for lavish grand opera and ballet. Concert-goers dress up to match.

Pesti Vigadó C 6
- M1 Vörösmarty tér
- V. Vigadó tér 2
- Tel. 318 9167

Orchestral music and occasional opera in a famous old theatre rebuilt after World War II bombing.

Thália Színház D 4
- M1 Oktogon
- VI. Nagymező utca 22–24
- Tel. 331 0500

Dance, theatre, opera, musicals in a stylish venue just off Andrássy út.

BARS, PUBS AND JAZZ BARS
Jazz and blues music plays in small bars and large pubs.

Banán Klub
- HÉV to Csillaghegy
- III. Mátyás Király utca 13–15
- Tel. 368 9049

Live bands and a good bar make this Óbuda's hottest nightspot.

Beckett's
- M3 Nyugati pu
- V. Bajcsy Zsilinszky út 72
- Tel. 311 1035

Budapest has no less than three Irish theme pubs. This one is a huge corner pub in the business district that's immensely popular with expats.

Darshan Café
- M3 Kálvin tér
- VIII. Krúdy Gyula utca 8
- Tel. 266 7797

Funky murals and psychedelic tiles create the right ambience for cool acid jazz and a laid-back crowd.

Erzsébet Híd Eszpresszó
- Tram 18
- I. Döbrentei tér 2
- Tel. 212 2127

On the Buda side of the Danube near Elizabeth Bridge, this bar has an outside terrace with great views.

Fat Mo's Club
- M2 Kálvin tér
- V. Nyári Pál. utca 9
- Tel. 267 3199
- Mon, Tues noon–2 a.m., Wed to 3 a.m.; Thurs, Fri to 4 a.m.; Sat 6 p.m.–4 a.m.; Sun 6 p.m.–2 a.m.

Tex-Mex specialities. America in the 1920s atmosphere.

Fonó Budai Zeneház
- Tram 47
- XI. Sztregova utca 3
- Tel. 206 5300

Superb bar some distance from the centre. Predominantly acoustic jazz and folk music, with *táncház—*

Transylvanian Dance House music—on Friday nights.

Fregatt Pub

- M3 Ferenciek tere
- V. Molnár utca 26
- Tél. 318 9997
- Mon–Sat 4 p.m.–1 a.m.

There's a friendly atmosphere in this Irish "frigate". Live concerts.

Grand Café Oktogon

- M1 Oktogon
- VI. Oktogon teréz korut 23
- Tel. 265 2935
- Daily 11 a.m.–midnight

Airy café in the traditional grand Budapest style. Franco-Hungarian cuisine. Live jazz Tues and Wed.

Incognito

- M1 Oktogon
- VI. Liszt Ferenc tér 3
- Tel. 342 1471
- Mon–Fri noon–midnight;
- Sat, Sun 2 p.m.–midnight

Cool atmosphere; the covers of classical jazz albums paper the walls.

Jazz Garden

- M3 Kálvin tér
- V. Veres Pálné utca 44/A
- Tel. 266 7364

Stylish club with high-quality live jazz. If you eat in the restaurant the cover charge will be deducted.

Old Man's Music Pub

- M2 Blaha Lujza tér
- VII. Akácfa utca 13
- Tel. 322 7645

Undoubtedly one of the best bars in Budapest, with an extensive menu, good service, nice decor and fine live blues and, less frequently, jazz bands, followed by a disco.

Piaf

- M1 Oktogon
- VI. Nagymezőutca 25
- Tel. 312 3823

Red velvet curtains and a photo of the eponymous *chanteuse* set the tone for the sophisticated jazz-oriented piano bar upstairs; exposed brickwork and a small dance floor in the intimate bar below.

Portside

- M2 Astoria
- VII. Dohány utca 7
- Tel. 351 8405

Pool tables, loud disco music and a mildly nautical theme pack in large crowds to this British-style pub.

Rózsadomb

- Tram 4, 6
- II. Bimbó utca 2
- Tel. 212 5512

Atmospherically downmarket bar, complete with formica tables and jukebox playing 1970s hits.

CLUBLAND

Budapest's clubs are best—for which read liveliest—at the weekend. The scene is generally more down-to-earth and certainly less expensive than its counterparts in London or Paris. There's a subtle distinction between music clubs—occasional live music, generally less obsessed with house and techno—and discos, which tend to offer a faster and louder experience.

Angel Club

M1 Vörösmarty utca or trolleybus 74 to Almássy tér
VII. Szövetség utca 33
Tel. 351 6490
Open Thurs–Sun

Budapest's biggest gay disco. Famous for the transvestite shows on Fridays and Saturdays at 11.30 p.m.

Music Club

M3 Nyugati pu
VI. Váci út 1
Tel. 302 4751

Wed–Sat 9 p.m.– 4 a.m.
Two large dance floors and an emphasis on rock and disco. It is

In bars and restaurants, there's plenty of old-fashioned entertainment, too.

frequented by expats and youngish Hungarians.

Café Capella
- M3 Ferenciek tere/Tram 2
- V. Belgrád rakpart 23
- Tel. 318 6231
- Thurs, Fri, Sat 9 p.m.–3 or 4 a.m.

Gay and mixed crowd in a lively cellar music club—the Saturday night drag show has become the stuff of legend.

Citadella Barfly Club
- Bus 27
- XI. Citadella sétány 2
- Tel. 209 3271
- Fri, Sat 10 p.m.–5 a.m.

On Gellért Hill, one of the few raver spots in the city, with the bonus of a view.

E-Klub
- M3 Népliget
- X. Népliget út 2
- Tel. 263 1614
- Fri, Sat 9 p.m.–5 a.m.

Immense complex with four rooms, with one devoted exclusively to 1980s music.

Trocadero
- M3 Nyugati pu
- V. Szent István körút 15
- Tel. 311 4691
- Mon–Thurs 9 p.m.–3 a.m.;
- Fri, Sat 9 p.m.–5 a.m.

Budapest's only Latin club. Branches out into reggae on Thursdays and soul music on Sundays.

CASINOS
Budapest's numerous casinos all offer French and American roulette, dice, poker, blackjack and punto banco. You'll need to obtain temporary membership, so don't forget your passport.

Budapest Hilton Hotel
- Shuttle bus from M2 Moszkva tér
- I. Hess András tér 1–3
- Tel. 375 1001
- Daily 7 p.m.–2 a.m.

The smartest casino in town, up on Buda hill.

Las Vegas
- Tram 2
- V. Roosevelt tér 2
- Tel. 266 2082
- Daily 2 p.m.–5 a.m.

A swish, upmarket operation located in the Atrium Hyatt Hotel.

Várkert
- Tram 19
- I. Ybl Miklós tér 9
- Tel. 202 4244
- Daily 2 p.m.–5 a.m.

You'll find locals and tourists alike huddled round the tables inside this splendid neo-Renaissance former pump-house of the Royal Palace.

The Hard Facts

Airport

All international flights land at Ferihegy airport, 24 km (15 miles) southeast of Budapest. There are two terminals, 2A and 2B (in the same building), with the smarter Terminal 2A being used mainly by Malév, the Hungarian national airline. The terminals provide currency exchange, car-hire and tourist information services, in addition to duty-free and refreshment facilities.

Probably the best way to get into town is to take the Airport Minibus which, for around 4,600 Ft return, will take you to your hotel. Tickets can be bought at the counter in the arrivals hall. To book the return journey, call 296 8555 the day before your departure.

The local 93 bus goes every 15 minutes to Kőbánya-Kispest metro station on the M3 blue line, from where it's a quick trip into the centre.

Taxis are of course found in abundance, and might be more economical than the Airport Minibus if there are more than two people travelling. But be sure to use a reputable firm or fix the price first, as passengers have been known to face extortionate charges by some taxi drivers. Airport Taxis (tel. 341 0000) offer a fixed rate, or else try one of the firms listed below under the Taxis heading.

Climate

The pleasant-sounding average summer temperature of 22°C (72°F) doesn't tell the whole story. The city can become very hot and humid, especially in July and August, a time when many locals head for the slightly cooler and certainly less-polluted shores of Lake Balaton. Winters are cold, although with a range of –4°C to +4°C (25°F to 39°F), they pack nothing like the icy punch of the Russian version. The best weather is to be found in May and September, when Budapest is pleasantly mild and still fairly crowd-free.

Communications

Post Offices are usually open Monday to Friday, 8 a.m.–6 p.m. The post offices at Keleti and Nyugati train stations, however, open daily 7 a.m.–9 p.m.

Telexes, telegrams and faxes can be sent from the larger offices. Stamps *(bélyeg)* may also be obtained at tobacconists, while hotels will generally post mail for you.

Telephone. To make overseas calls from Budapest, dial 00 then the country code and number.

Country code for Canada and US is 1, for UK 44. For national calls outside Budapest you must first dial the access code 06 then the area code and number.

The international code for Hungary is 36, the area code for Budapest is 1. To call Budapest from abroad dial 00 36 + 1 + the seven-digit number.

Hungary's telephone system is operated by the Magyar Telekom Group (T-Com and T-Mobile. Local and international calls can be made from public telephone boxes. Phone cards are on sale at post offices, newsagents and hotels. Payphones accept Euro coins. The telecommunications centre at Petőfi Sándor utca 17 (tel. 317 5500) offers an efficient phone, fax and telex service.

Useful numbers:
International operator: 190
International Directory
    Enquiries: 199
Domestic Directory Enquiries:
    198
English is spoken on all three services

Customs

The allowance for duty-free importation of goods into Hungary for passengers from non-EU countries is 200 cigarettes or 50 cigars or 250 grams of tobacco, one litre of spirits and two litres of wine.

You can import and export up to 200,000 forint.

Disabled

Budapest's grand old galleries and museums aren't exactly easy places for disabled travellers to negotiate, but the city authorities are working hard to improve things, with access now possible to the Museum of Fine Arts and the Museum of Applied Arts, for example. Unfortunately, public transport, other than the M1 metro line and the Airport Minibus, continues to pose a considerable challenge.

For more information, contact the Hungarian Disabled Association (MEOSZ), tel. 388 8951, e-mail: meosz@axelero.hu.

Driving

Driving around Budapest is something of a non-starter: the roads are crowded and often in bad condition, Hungarian drivers are notably lackadaisical about traffic regulations and parking is a nightmare. Nagivation is difficult if you are not familiar with the city as there are no left turns: you either turn right or drive straight on. (So don't get angry with your taxi driver if he seems to be going in circles; it's the only way). On top of this, the city has an extensive public transport system, the city centre is eminently walkable and traffic is banned altogether from Castle Hill (unless you are staying at the Hilton).

If you do need to drive around Budapest, watch out for trams, which hurtle along the main boulevards, and pay special attention to people alighting from them in the middle of the road. Never leave anything of value in the car when it's parked. If the car has disappeared when you return, it may have been towed, in which case contact the local police station. The central station is at Szalay utca 11–13. There are multi-storey car parks at Bárczy István utca 2 and Türr István utca 5, all in district V.

Outside Budapest you will find a good, toll-free motorway network, and if you plan to do a lot of touring, a car can make things easier than getting around by bus and train. If you bring your own car, make sure you have your passport, driving licence, car registration document and insurance certificate with you at all times.

Alternatively, you can hire a car when you arrive in Budapest. All the big car-hire firms have offices at the airport and in town. Local companies may be a less expensive option. You'll need to show a valid driving licence, be over 21 (in most cases), and have a credit card for the deposit. Prices vary and it pays to compare the deals on offer. Make sure the amount agreed upon includes the 25% ÁFA sales tax (VAT) and insurance, and establish what mileage you are allowed, or else you'll get a shock when the final bill is presented.

Avis:
  Szervita tér 8
  tel. 1 318 4240

Europcar:
  Deák tér 3
  tel. 1 3286465

Sixt:
  Konyves Kalman krt 5
  tel. 1 451 4220
  enquiries: 0870 156 75 67

When driving, keep to the right and overtake on the left. Wearing seatbelts is compulsory and drinking and driving is illegal, with heavy penalties for those found guilty. Car headlights must be switched on even during the day.

Petrol stations are ubiquitous along the motorways and main roads. The bigger ones are self-service and take credit cards. Unleaded fuel is *ólommentes*, leaded is *benzin*, oil is *olaj*.

Speed limits are: 120 kph (75 mph) on motorways; 100 kph (62 mph) on dual carriageways; 80 kph (50 mph) on other roads; and 50 kph (30 mph) in built-up areas.

terCard using your regular PIN code. Do not change money in the street.

Credit cards are widely accepted, especially in larger hotels, restaurants and shops. Some petrol stations may still insist on cash, so be sure to have enough if driving outside the city at weekends, for example.

Currency. The Forint (Ft or HUF) is issued in coins of 1, 2, 5, 10, 20, 50 and 100 Ft, and banknotes of 200, 500, 1,000, 2,000, 5,000, 10,000 and 20,000 Ft. US dollars are widely accepted, even on market stalls.

Travellers cheques are easily changed at banks and exchange bureaux with passport identification, but cash usually guarantees a better rate.

Public Holidays

January 1	New Year's Day
March 15	Anniversary of 1848 Revolution
May 1	Labour Day
August 20	St Stephen's Day
October 23	Anniversary of 1956 Uprising and 1989 establishment of the Republic
November 1	All Saints' Day
December 25 and 26	Christmas
Moveable:	Easter Monday Whit Monday

Public Transport

Note that you can make savings on transport by investing in the Budapest Card (see p. 15).

The Budapest Transport Company (BKV) runs a large network of buses, trams and trolleybuses as well as three metro lines and, in summer, a ferry service on the Danube. The system is efficient, reliable, extremely good value and gets you within walking distance of just about all the main sights. Most public transport starts at around 4.30 a.m. and goes on till 11.30 p.m. There's a limited night service, denoted by the letter É after bus and tram numbers. Maps of the system can be bought at the main metro and railway stations.

BKV tickets (*jegy*) are valid across the whole network and are available at stations, newsstands, and travel offices. You can buy a single ticket or carnets of 10 or 20, which work out cheaper. Tickets must be validated for each journey or you may face an on-the-spot fine (inspectors are plain-clothed and will suddenly slip on a red armband before asking for your ticket). Buses and trams have red ticket-punching machines on board, but on the metro you'll need to use the orange machines inside the station entrance before boarding the train. Note that one ticket is valid for only one ride (you'll need a new ticket even if you change metro trains). Alternatively you can get a 1-, 3-, 7-, 14- or 30-day pass, which can be used for an unlimited number of journeys across the network, though for anything more than the 1- and 3-day passes you'll need a passport-size photograph.

BKV tickets are valid on the overground HÉV line within the city limits. If you're heading up to Szentendre, for example, you'll need to pay a supplementary fare.

Some of Budapest's more unusual conveyances, such as the Children's Railway and the Castle Hill funicular, are separate from the BKV network and are not covered by its tickets and passes, but you can still get to Buda Castle by the less scenic BKV Várbusz shuttle bus, which leaves from Moszkva tér.

Safety

Although crime levels have risen since the fall of communism, Budapest remains a fairly safe city by Western standards. It is nonetheless worth taking some basic precautions. Only carry the money you will need for the day along with a credit card. Deposit traveller's cheques, plane tickets, valuables, etc., in the hotel safe if possible. Watch out for pickpockets in crowded tourist areas and on public transport,

and beware of scams aimed at foreigners along Váci utca, which will always end up with you and your money parting company.

Tax Refund

A sales tax of 16 per cent is imposed on goods in Hungary. To benefit from a tax refund, your purchase in any one store must amount to a minimum of 50,000 Ft. Ask the sales assistant for a fiscal invoice, a VAT Reclaim form and a tax-free envelope. Keep all receipts for currency exchange and your credit card slips, and when you leave the country, have all these documents stamped by a Hungarian Customs Officer. Shops offering this service display a Tax-free Shopping logo. More information on www.globalrefund.com

Taxis

With such a superb public transport system, you probably won't have much call for Budapest's taxis, which means you'll miss the chance to witness the drivers' notorious skills in creative fare-charging. But should you find yourself in need of one, the following are acknowledged as the more reputable firms:

City Taxi	Tel. 211 1111
Fő Taxi	Tel. 222 2222
Tele5	Tel. 355 5555
Volán Taxi	Tel. 466 6666

Time
GMT + 1 (GMT + 2 in summer).

Tipping
Some restaurants have taken to levying a 10% service charge, in which case you might not wish to add any more. Most don't, though, and it is usual to round the bill up or leave a 10% tip, something which applies to taxi drivers as well. It is also customary to give a gratuity to doormen, porters, attendants and masseuses in baths, toilet and cloakroom attendants and theatre ushers.

Toilets
The city is well stocked with public toilets. There's usually an attendant on call and there will be a small charge. Otherwise, nip into a big hotel or make use of the facilities at museums, restaurants and coffee houses. *Férfiak* means "men" and *Nők* means "women".

Tourist Information
The two officially sanctioned tourist agencies are IBUSZ and Tourinform. The staff are helpful, speak English and provide useful information on accommodation, cultural events, opening times and so on.

Tourinform (head office)
V. Deak tér (Sütő utca 2)
Tel. 438 8080

www.tourinform.hu
mail: hungary@tourinform.hu
Mon–Fri 9 a.m.–7 p.m.
Sat–Sun 9 a.m.–4 p.m.

IBUSZ
V. Ferenciek tere 10
Tel. 485 27 00
mail: i038@ibusz.hu
Mon–Fri 9 a.m.–6 p.m.
Sat 9 a.m.–1 p.m.

Voltage
Electric current is 220 volts, and sockets are for plugs with two round pins. British and American equipment will need an adaptor.

Websites
For online information about Budapest and Hungary:

www.budapestinfo.hu
  The city's official website

www.budapestsun.com
  News coverage in English

www.insidehungary.com
  News and current affairs

www.tex.hu
  Ticket Express: cultural events

www.budapestweek.hu
  Listings of cultural events

www.hungary.com
www.itthon.hu
  Tourist information

www.szotar-sztaki.hu
  English-Hungarian dictionary

GENERAL EDITOR
  Barbara Ender-Jones
EDITOR
  Christina Grisewood
RESEARCH
  Judit Hollos Spoerli
LAYOUT
  Luc Malherbe
PHOTO CREDITS
  Wysocki/hemis.fr:
  front cover,
  pp. 1, 2, 5, 6, 10, 17, 22, 43;
  Rieger/hemis.fr: p. 25;
  Gardel/hemis.fr: p. 50;
  VISA/Louvet: p. 28;
  VISA/Cleek: pp. 31, 34;
  Marguerite Martinoli:
  pp. 47, 59, 69;
  Claude Huber: p. 55
MAPS
  Huber Kartographie;
  Elsner & Schichor

Copyright © 2006, 2001
by JPM Publications S.A.
12, avenue William-Fraisse,
1006 Lausanne, Switzerland
information@jpmguides.com
http://www.jpmguides.com/

Printed in Switzerland
Weber/Bienne (CTP)
10016.00.0210
Edition 2006–2007

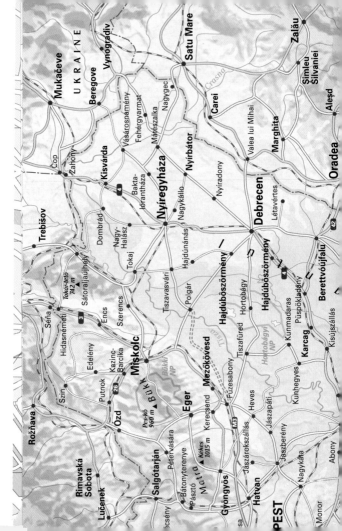

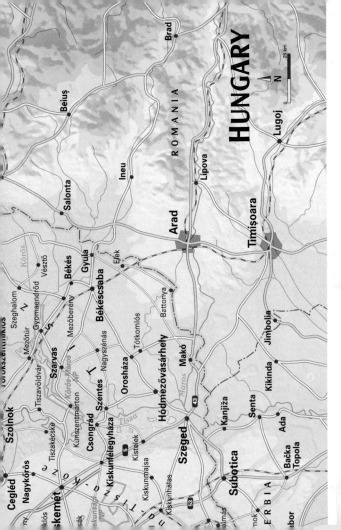